PRAISE FOR ROBIN SHARMA AND

The Monk Who Sold His Ferrari

'Robin Sharma's books are helping people all over the world live great lives.' – Paulo Coelho, #1 bestselling author of *The Alchemist*

'Robin Sharma has the rare gift of writing books that are truly life-changing.' – Richard Carlson, Ph.D., author of the #1 *New York Times* bestseller *Don't Sweat the Small Stuff*

'Nothing less than sensational. This book will bless your life.' – Mark Victor Hansen, co-author, *Chicken Soup for the Soul*

'A great book, from an inspirational point of view.' – Carlos Delgado, Major League baseball superstar

'This is a fun, fascinating, fanciful adventure into the realms of personal development, personal effectiveness and individual happiness. It contains treasures of wisdom that can enrich and enhance the life of every single person.' – Brian Tracy, author of *Maximum Achievement*

'Robin S. Sharma has an important message for all of us – one that can change our lives. He's written a one-of-a-kind handbook for person
– Scott DeGarmo, past

'The book is about finding out what is truly important to your real spiritual self, rather than being inundated with material possessions.' – Michelle Yeoh, lead actress of *Crouching Tiger, Hidden Dragon*, in *TIME* Magazine

'Robin Sharma has created an enchanting tale that incorporates the classic tools of transformation into a simple philosophy of living. A delightful book that will change your life.' – Elaine St. James, author of *Simplify Your Life* and *Inner Simplicity*

'Sheds light on life's big questions.' – *The Edmonton Journal*

'*The Monk Who Sold His Ferrari* is coherent, useful and definitely worth reading … It can truly help readers cope with the rat race.' – *The Kingston Whig-Standard*

'Simple wisdom that anyone can benefit from.' – *The Calgary Herald*

'This book could be classified as *The Wealthy Barber* of personal development … [It contains] insightful messages on the key concepts which help bring greater balance, control and effectiveness in our daily lives.' – *Investment Executive*

'A treasure – an elegant and powerful formula for true success and happiness. Robin S. Sharma has captured the wisdom of the ages and made it relevant for these turbulent times. I couldn't put it down.' – Joe Tye, author of *Never Fear, Never Quit*

'Simple rules for reaching one's potential.' – *The Halifax Daily News*

'Sharma guides readers toward enlightenment.' – *The Chronicle-Herald*

'A wonderfully crafted parable revealing a set of simple yet surprisingly potent ideas for improving the quality of anyone's life. I'm recommending this gem of a book to all of my clients.' – George Williams, president, Karat Consulting International

'Robin Sharma offers personal fulfillment along the spiritual highroad.' – *Ottawa Citizen*

PRAISE FOR

Leadership Wisdom from
The Monk Who Sold His Ferrari

'One of the year's best business books.' – *PROFIT Magazine*

'Very informative, easy to read and extremely helpful … We have distributed copies to all our management team as well as to store operators. The feedback has been very positive.' – David Bloom, CEO, Shoppers Drug Mart

'Robin Sharma has a neat, down-to-earth way of expressing his powerful solutions for today's most pressing leadership issues. This is so refreshing in a period when businesspeople are faced with so much jargon.' – Ian Turner, manager, Celestica Learning Centre

'This book is a gold mine of wisdom and common sense.' – Dean Larry Tapp, Richard Ivey School of Business, University of Western Ontario

'A terrific book that will help any businessperson lead and live more effectively.' – Jim O'Neill, director of operations, District Sales Division, London Life

'Sharma's mission is to provide the reader with the insight to become a visionary leader, helping them transform their business into an organization that thrives in this era of change.' – *Sales Promotion Magazine*

Life Lessons

from the

Monk who Sold his Ferrari

Robin Sharma

Life Lessons

from the

Monk who sold his Ferrari

Thorsons

Thorsons
An imprint of HarperCollins*Publishers*
1 London Bridge Street
London SE1 9GF

www.harpercollins.co.uk

HarperCollins*Publishers*
1st Floor, Watermarque Building, Ringsend Road
Dublin 4, Ireland

First published as *Who Will Cry When You Die?*
by HarperCollins*Publishers* Ltd 1999

This edition published by Thorsons 2014

11

© Robin Sharma 1999

Robin S. Sharma asserts the moral right to
be identified as the author of this work

A catalogue record of this book is
available from the British Library

ISBN: 978-0-00-754960-3

Printed and bound by CPI Group (UK),
Croydon CR0 4YY

MIX
Paper from
responsible sources
FSC™ C007454

This book is produced from independently certified FSC™ paper
to ensure responsible forest management.

For more information visit: www.harpercollins.co.uk/green

I dedicate this book to you, the reader. May you apply the life lessons you discover within these pages to manifest the fullness of your talents while making a difference in the lives of all those around you.

This book is also dedicated to my children, Colby and Bianca, two of my greatest teachers. I love you.

The tragedy of life is not death, but what we let
die inside of us while we live.
– Norman Cousins

Contents

	Foreword	xv
	Preface	xvii
1.	Discover Your Calling	1
2.	Every Day, Be Kind to a Stranger	4
3.	Maintain Your Perspective	6
4.	Practice Tough Love	8
5.	Keep a Journal	10
6.	Develop an Honesty Philosophy	12
7.	Honor Your Past	14
8.	Start Your Day Well	16
9.	Learn to Say No Gracefully	18
10.	Take a Weekly Sabbatical	20
11.	Talk to Yourself	22
12.	Schedule Worry Breaks	24
13.	Model a Child	27
14.	Remember, Genius Is 99 Percent Inspiration	29
15.	Care for the Temple	31
16.	Learn to Be Silent	33

17. Think About Your Ideal Neighborhood   35
18. Get Up Early   37
19. See Your Troubles as Blessings   40
20. Laugh More   42
21. Spend a Day Without Your Watch   44
22. Take More Risks   46
23. Live a Life   49
24. Learn from a Good Movie   51
25. Bless Your Money   53
26. Focus on the Worthy   55
27. Write Thank-You Notes   58
28. Always Carry a Book with You   60
29. Create a Love Account   63
30. Get Behind People's Eyeballs   65
31. List Your Problems   67
32. Practice the Action Habit   69
33. See Your Children as Gifts   71
34. Enjoy the Path, Not Just the Reward   73
35. Remember That Awareness Precedes Change   75
36. Read *Tuesdays with Morrie*   77
37. Master Your Time   79
38. Keep Your Cool   81
39. Recruit a Board of Directors   83
40. Cure Your Monkey Mind   85
41. Get Good at Asking   87
42. Look for the Higher Meaning of Your Work   89
43. Build a Library of Heroic Books   91
44. Develop Your Talents   94
45. Connect with Nature   97
46. Use Your Commute Time   99
47. Go on a News Fast   101
48. Get Serious About Setting Goals   103

49. Remember the Rule of 21   105
50. Practice Forgiveness   107
51. Drink Fresh Fruit Juice   109
52. Create a Pure Environment   111
53. Walk in the Woods   113
54. Get a Coach   115
55. Take a Mini-Vacation   117
56. Become a Volunteer   119
57. Find Your Six Degrees of Separation   121
58. Listen to Music Daily   123
59. Write a Legacy Statement   125
60. Find Three Great Friends   127
61. Read *The Artist's Way*   129
62. Learn to Meditate   131
63. Have a Living Funeral   133
64. Stop Complaining and Start Living   135
65. Increase Your Value   137
66. Be a Better Parent   139
67. Be Unorthodox   141
68. Carry a Goal Card   143
69. Be More than Your Moods   145
70. Savor the Simple Stuff   147
71. Stop Condemning   149
72. See Your Day as Your Life   151
73. Create a Master Mind Alliance   153
74. Create a Daily Code of Conduct   155
75. Imagine a Richer Reality   157
76. Become the CEO of Your Life   159
77. Be Humble   162
78. Don't Finish Every Book You Start   164
79. Don't Be So Hard on Yourself   166
80. Make a Vow of Silence   168

81. Don't Pick Up the Phone Every Time It Rings   170
82. Remember That Recreation Must
    Involve Re-creation   172
83. Choose Worthy Opponents   173
84. Sleep Less   175
85. Have a Family Mealtime   178
86. Become an Imposter   180
87. Take a Public Speaking Course   182
88. Stop Thinking Tiny Thoughts   184
89. Don't Worry About Things You Can't Change   186
90. Learn How to Walk   187
91. Rewrite Your Life Story   189
92. Plant a Tree   191
93. Find Your Place of Peace   193
94. Take More Pictures   195
95. Be an Adventurer   197
96. Decompress Before You Go Home   198
97. Respect Your Instincts   200
98. Collect Quotes That Inspire You   202
99. Love Your Work   204
100. Selflessly Serve   206
101. Live Fully so You Can Die Happy   208

Acknowledgments   211

FOREWORD

It's a true privilege to be able to write this message to you as you begin this very special edition of *Life Lessons from the Monk Who Sold His Ferrari*.

I wrote this book during a hard time in my life. And so I was going deep, highly reflective and doing my very best to understand what makes a human life happy, excellent and peaceful. As you know, adversity is a superb servant, helping us strip away the distractions and shiny toys of the world to refocus us on what's truly important. And it reminds us about the pursuits that truly matter.

Life Lessons from the Monk Who Sold His Ferrari is a powerful manual for living your absolute best life. The chapters are short, enormously practical and hopefully truly inspiring. And the ideas I share, while simple, are ultimately game-changing once you have the courage to act on them and make them a part of your daily habits. Today could be the first day of your greatest life. I'm very excited for you.

More than anything else, I wrote this book to help you break free of any shackles that may be holding you back from expressing the potential that you were born into, so that you get big things done, experience a remarkable sense of joy that lasts and live a life that's truly legendary. Yes, legendary.

So enjoy – and savor – the insights that follow. Make the course corrections you're ready to make. And inspire everyone who is blessed to intersect with your path by the person that I know you'll step into being.

Your fan,
Robin Sharma

P.S. I love connecting with my readers at robinsharma.com. You'll also find a wealth of training videos, free ebooks, podcasts and other learning resources that will help your transformation. And keep you energized. Again, my best wishes.

PREFACE

I honor you for picking up this book. In doing so, you have
made the decision to live more deliberately, more joyfully
and completely. You have decided to live your life by choice
rather than by chance, by design rather than by default.
And for this, I applaud you.

Since writing the two previous books in *The Monk Who
Sold His Ferrari* series, I have received countless letters from
readers who saw their lives change through the wisdom
they discovered. The comments of these men and women
inspired and moved me. Many of the notes I received also
encouraged me to distill all that I have learned about the
art of living into a series of life lessons. And so, I set about
compiling the best I have to give into a book that I truly
believe will help transform your life.

The words on the following pages are heartfelt and written in the high hope that you will not only connect with the
wisdom I respectfully offer but act on it to create lasting

improvements in every life area. Through my own trials, I have found that it is not enough to know what to do – we must act on that knowledge in order to have the lives we want.

And so as you turn the pages of this third book in *The Monk Who Sold His Ferrari* series, I hope you will discover a wealth of wisdom that will enrich the quality of your professional, personal and spiritual life. Please do write to me, send me an e-mail or visit with me at one of my seminars to share how you have integrated the lessons in this book into the way you live. I will do my very best to respond to your letters with a personal note. I wish you deep peace, great prosperity and many happy days spent engaged in a worthy purpose.

Robin Sharma

1.

DISCOVER YOUR
CALLING

⟨⟨ ⟩⟩

When I was growing up, my father said something to me I will never forget, 'Son, when you were born, you cried while the world rejoiced. Live your life in such a way that when you die the world cries while you rejoice.' We live in an age when we have forgotten what life is all about. We can easily put a person on the Moon, but we have trouble walking across the street to meet a new neighbor. We can fire a missile across the world with pinpoint accuracy, but we have trouble keeping a date with our children to go to the library. We have e-mail, fax machines and digital phones so that we can stay connected and yet we live in a time where human beings have never been less connected. We have lost touch with our humanity. We have lost touch with our purpose. We have lost sight of the things that matter the most.

And so, as you start this book, I respectfully ask you, Who will cry when you die? How many lives will you touch while you have the privilege to walk this planet? What impact will your life have on the generations that follow you? And what legacy will you leave behind after you have taken your last breath? One of the lessons I have learned in my own life is that if you don't act on life, life has a habit of acting on you. The days slip into weeks, the weeks slip into months and the months slip into years. Pretty soon it's all over and you are left with nothing more than a heart filled with regret over a life half lived. George Bernard Shaw was asked on his deathbed, 'What would you do if you could live your life over again?' He reflected, then replied with a deep sigh: 'I'd like to be the person I could have been but never was.' I've written this book so that this will never happen to you.

As a professional speaker, I spend much of my work life delivering keynote addresses at conferences across North America, flying from city to city, sharing my insights on leadership in business and in life with many different people. Though they all come from diverse walks of life, their questions invariably center on the same things these days: How can I find greater meaning in my life? How can I make a lasting contribution through my work? and How can I simplify so that I can enjoy the journey of life before it is too late?

My answer always begins the same way: Find your calling. I believe we all have special talents that are just waiting to be engaged in a worthy pursuit. We are all here for some unique purpose, some noble objective that will allow us to manifest our highest human potential while we, at the same time, add value to the lives around us. Finding your calling doesn't mean you must leave the job you now have. It simply means you need to bring more of yourself into your work and focus on the things you do best. It means you have to stop waiting for other people to make the changes you desire and, as Mahatma Gandhi noted: 'Be the change that you wish to see most in your world.' And once you do, your life will change.

2.

EVERY DAY, BE KIND
TO A STRANGER

On his deathbed, Aldous Huxley reflected on his entire life's learning and then summed it up in seven simple words: 'Let us be kinder to one another.' All too often, we believe that in order to live a truly fulfilling life we must achieve some great act or grand feat that will put us on the front covers of magazines and newspapers. Nothing could be further from the truth. A meaningful life is made up of a series of daily acts of decency and kindness, which, ironically, add up to something truly great over the course of a lifetime.

Everyone who enters your life has a lesson to teach and a story to tell. Every person you pass during the moments that make up your days represents an opportunity to show a little more of the compassion and courtesy that define your humanity. Why not start being more of the person you truly are during your days and doing what you can to enrich the world around you? In my mind, if you make even one person smile during your day or brighten the mood of even one stranger, your day has been a worthwhile one. Kindness, quite simply, is the rent we must pay for the space we occupy on this planet.

Become more creative in the ways you show compassion to strangers. Paying the toll for the person in the car behind you, offering your seat on the subway to someone in need and being the first to say hello are great places to start. Recently, I received a letter from a reader of *The Monk Who Sold His Ferrari* who lives in Washington State. In it she wrote: 'I have a practice of tithing to people who have helped me along my spiritual path. Please accept the enclosed check of $100 with my blessing and gratitude.' I quickly responded to her generous act by sending one of my audiotape programs in return so she received value for the gift she sent me. Her gesture was a great lesson in the importance of giving sincerely and from the heart.

3.

MAINTAIN YOUR PERSPECTIVE

<< • >>

One day, according to an old story, a man with a serious illness was wheeled into a hospital room where another patient was resting on a bed next to the window. As the two became friends, the one next to the window would look out of it and then spend the next few hours delighting his bedridden companion with vivid descriptions of the world outside. Some days he would describe the beauty of the trees in the park across from the hospital and how the leaves danced in the wind. On other days, he would entertain his friend with step-by-step replays of the things people were doing as they walked by the hospital. However, as time went on, the bedridden man grew frustrated at his inability to observe the wonders his friend described. Eventually he grew to dislike him and then to hate him intensely.

One night, during a particularly bad coughing fit, the patient next to the window stopped breathing. Rather than pressing the button for help, the other man chose to do nothing. The next morning the patient who had given his friend so much happiness by recounting the sights outside the window was pronounced dead and wheeled out of the hospital room. The other man quickly asked that his bed be placed next to the window, a request that was complied with by the attending nurse. But as he looked out the window, he discovered something that made him shake: the window faced a stark brick wall. His former roommate had conjured up the incredible sights that he described in his imagination as a loving gesture to make the world of his friend a little bit better during a difficult time. He had acted out of selfless love.

This story never fails to create a shift in my own perspective when I think about it. To live happier, more fulfilling lives, when we encounter a difficult circumstance, we must keep shifting our perspective and continually ask ourselves, 'Is there a wiser, more enlightened way of looking at this seemingly negative situation?' Stephen Hawking, one of the greatest physicists ever, is reported to have said that we live on a minor planet of a very average star located within the outer limits of one of a hundred thousand million galaxies. How's that for a shift in perspective? Given this information, are your troubles really that big? Are the problems you have experienced or the challenges you might currently be facing really as serious as you have made them out to be?

We walk this planet for such a short time. In the overall scheme of things, our lives are mere blips on the canvas of eternity. So have the wisdom to enjoy the journey and savor the process.

4.

PRACTICE TOUGH LOVE

The golden thread of a highly successful and meaningful life is self-discipline. Discipline allows you to do all those things you know in your heart you should do but never feel like doing. Without self-discipline, you will not set clear goals, manage your time effectively, treat people well, persist through the tough times, care for your health or think positive thoughts.

I call the habit of self-discipline 'Tough Love' because getting tough with yourself is actually a very loving gesture. By being stricter with yourself, you will begin to live life more deliberately, on your own terms rather than simply reacting to life the way a leaf floating in a stream drifts according to the flow of the current on a particular day. As I teach in one of my seminars, the tougher you are on yourself, the easier life will be on you. The quality of your life ultimately is shaped by the quality of your choices and decisions, ones that range from the career you choose to pursue to the books you read, the time that you wake up every morning and the thoughts you think during the hours of your days. When you consistently flex your will-power by making those choices that you know are the right ones (rather than the easy ones), you take back control of your life. Effective, fulfilled people do not spend their time doing what is most convenient and comfortable. They have the courage to listen to their hearts and to do the wise thing. This habit is what makes them great.

'The successful person has the habit of doing the things failures don't like to do,' remarked essayist and thinker E. M. Gray. 'They don't like doing them either, necessarily. But their disliking is subordinated to the strength of their purpose.' The nineteenth-century English writer Thomas Henry Huxley arrived at a similar conclusion, noting: 'Perhaps the most valuable result of all education is the ability to make yourself do the thing you have to do, when it ought to be done, whether you like it or not.' And Aristotle made this point of wisdom in yet another way: 'Whatever we learn to do, we learn by actually doing it: men come to be builders, for instance, by building, and harp players, by playing the harp. In the same way, by doing just acts we come to be just; by doing self-controlled acts, we come to be self-controlled; and by doing brave acts, we come to be brave.'

5.

Keep a Journal

Maintaining a daily journal is one of the best personal growth initiatives you will ever take. Writing down your daily experiences along with the lessons you have drawn from them will make you wiser with each passing day. You will develop self-awareness and make fewer mistakes. And keeping a journal will help clarify your intentions so that you remain focused on the things that truly count.

Writing in a journal offers you the opportunity to have regular one-on-one conversations with yourself. It forces you to do some deep thinking in a world where deep thinking is a thing of the past. It will also make you a clearer thinker and help you live in a more intentional and enlightened way. In addition, it provides a central place where you can record your insights on important issues, note key success strategies that have worked for you and commit to all those things you know are important to achieve for a high-quality professional, personal and spiritual life. And your personal journal gives you a private place to flex your imagination and define your dreams.

A journal is not a diary. A diary is a place where you record events while a journal is a place where you analyze and evaluate them. Keeping a journal encourages you to consider what you do, why you do it and what you have learned from all you have done. And writing in a journal promotes personal growth and wisdom by giving you a forum to study, and then leverage, your past for greater success in your future. Medical researchers have even found that writing in a private journal for as little time as 15 minutes a day can improve health, functioning of your immune system and your overall attitude. Remember, if your life is worth thinking about, it is worth writing about.

6.

DEVELOP AN
HONESTY PHILOSOPHY

We live in a world of broken promises. We live in a time when people treat their words lightly. We tell a friend we will call her next week for lunch knowing full well we do not have the time to do so. We promise a co-worker we will bring in that new book we love so much knowing full well that we never lend out our books. And we promise ourselves this will be the year we will get back into shape, simplify our lives and have more fun without any real intention of making the deep life changes necessary to achieve these goals.

Saying things we don't really mean becomes a habit when we practice it long enough. The real problem is that when you don't keep your word, you lose credibility. When you lose credibility, you break the bonds of trust. And breaking the bonds of trust ultimately leads to a string of broken relationships.

To develop an honesty philosophy, begin to monitor how many small untruths you tell over the course of a week. Go on what I call a 'truth fast' for the next seven days and vow to be completely honest in all your dealings with others – and with yourself. Every time you fail to do the right thing, you fuel the habit of doing the wrong thing. Every time you do not tell the truth, you feed the habit of being untruthful. When you promise someone you will do something, do it. Be a person of your word rather than being 'all talk and no action'. As Mother Teresa said, 'there should be less talk; a preaching point is not a meeting point. What do you do then? Take a broom and clean someone's house. That says enough.'

7.

HONOR YOUR PAST

Every second you dwell on the past you steal from your future. Every minute you spend focusing on your problems you take away from finding your solutions. And thinking about all those things that you wish never happened to you is actually blocking all the things you want to happen from entering into your life. Given the timeless truth that holds that you become what you think about all day long, it makes no sense to worry about past events or mistakes unless you want to experience them for a second time. Instead, use the lessons you have learned from your past to rise to a whole new level of awareness and enlightenment.

Life's greatest setbacks reveal life's biggest opportunities. As the ancient thinker Euripides noted, 'There is in the worst of fortune the best chances for a happy change.' If you have suffered more than your fair share of difficulties in life, perhaps you are being prepared to serve some greater purpose that will require you to be equipped with the wisdom you have acquired through your trials. Use these life lessons to fuel your future growth. Remember, happy people have often experienced as much adversity as those who are unhappy. What sets them apart is that they have the good sense to manage their memories in a way that enriches their lives.

And understand that if you have failed more than others, there is a very good chance you are living more completely than others. Those who take more chances and dare to be more and do more than others will naturally experience more failures. But personally, I would rather have the bravery to try something and then fail than never to have tried it at all. I would much prefer spending the rest of my days expanding my human frontiers and trying to make the seemingly impossible probable than live a life of comfort, security and mediocrity. That's the essence of true life success. As Herodotus noted so sagely, 'It is better by noble boldness to run the risk of being subject to half of the evils we anticipate than to remain in cowardly listlessness for fear of what may happen.' Or as Booker T. Washington said, 'I have learned that success is to be measured not so much by the position that one has reached in life as by the obstacles he has overcome while trying to succeed.'

8.

START YOUR DAY WELL

<< >>

The way you begin your day determines the way you will live your day. I call the first thirty minutes after you wake up 'The Platinum 30' since they are truly the most valuable moments of your day and have a profound influence on the quality of every minute that follows. If you have the wisdom and self-discipline to ensure that, during this key period, you think only the purest of thoughts and take only the finest of actions, you will notice that your days will consistently unfold in the most marvelous ways.

Recently, I took my two young children to see the thrilling IMAX movie *Everest*. Aside from the breathtaking imagery and the powerful acts of heroism portrayed, there was one point that stayed with me: in order for the mountain-climbers to scale the summit, it was essential for them to have a good base camp. It was impossible for them to get to the top without that camp at the bottom that offered them a sanctuary for rest, renewal and replenishing. Once

16

they reached Camp Two, they then returned to the base for a few weeks to recharge their batteries. On reaching Camp Three, they hastily retreated to base camp to prepare for the trek to Camp Four. And on reaching Camp Four, they again went back down the mountain to base camp before making their final push for the summit. In the same way, I think that every one of us, in order to reach our personal summits and master the daily challenges of our own lives, needs to revisit our base camps during 'The Platinum 30'. We need to go to a place where we can reconnect to our life's mission, renew our selves and refocus on the things that matter most.

In my own life, I have developed a very effective morning ritual that consistently gets my day off to a joyful and peace-filled start. After waking, I head down to my 'personal sanctuary', a little space I have created for myself where I can practice my renewal activities without being disturbed. I then spend about fifteen minutes in silent contemplation, focusing on all the good things in my life and envisioning the day that I expect is about to unfold. Next I pick up a book from the wisdom literature, one rich with those time-less truths of successful living that are so easy to forget in these fast-paced times we live in. Examples include *Meditations* by the Roman philosopher Marcus Aurelius, *The Autobiography of Benjamin Franklin*, and *Walden* by Henry David Thoreau. The lessons in these works center me on the things that truly count and help launch my day on the right footing. And the wisdom I read during that precious early morning period infuses and enlightens every remaining minute of my day. So start your day well. You will never be the same.

9.

LEARN TO SAY
NO GRACEFULLY

It is easy to say yes to every request on your time when the priorities of your life are unclear. When your days are not guided by a rich and inspiring vision for your future, a clear image of an end result that will help you act more intentionally, it is not hard for the agendas of those around you to dictate your actions. As I wrote in *Leadership Wisdom from The Monk Who Sold His Ferrari*, 'if your priorities don't get scheduled into your planner, other people's priorities will get put into your planner.' The solution is to be clear about your life's highest objectives and then to learn to say no with grace.

The Chinese sage Chuang-tzu told the story of a man who forged swords for a maharaja. Even at the age of ninety, his work was carried out with exceptional precision and ability. No matter how rushed he was, he never made even the slightest slip. One day, the maharaja asked the old man, 'Is this a natural talent or is there some special technique that you use to create your remarkable results?' 'It is concentration on the essentials,' replied the sword-crafter. 'I took to forging swords when I was twenty-one years old. I did not care about anything else. If it was not a sword, I did not look at it or pay any attention to it. Forging swords became my passion and my purpose. I took all the energy that I did not give in other directions and put it in the direction of my art. This is the secret to my mastery.'

The most effective people concentrate on their 'areas of excellence', that is, on the things they do best and on those high-impact activities that will advance their lifework. In being so consumed by the important things, they find it easy to say no to the less-than-worthy distractions that clamor for their attention. Michael Jordan, the best basketball player in the game's history, did not negotiate his contracts, design his uniforms and prepare his travel schedules. He focused his time and energies on what he did best: playing basketball, and delegated everything else to his handlers. Jazz great Louis Armstrong did not spend his time selling tickets to his shows and setting up chairs for the audience. He concentrated on his point of brilliance: playing the trumpet. Learning to say no to the non-essentials will give you more time to devote to the things that have the power to truly improve the way you live and help you leave the legacy you know in your heart you are destined to leave.

10.

TAKE A WEEKLY
SABBATICAL

$\subset\subset\ \gg$

In ancient days, the seventh day of the week was known as the Sabbath. Reserved for some of life's most important yet commonly neglected pursuits, including spending time with one's family and hours in deep reflection and self-renewal, it provided a chance for hard-working people to renew their batteries and spend a day living life more fully. However, as the pace of life quickened and more activities began to compete for people's attention, this wonderful tradition was lost along with the tremendous personal benefits that flowed from it.

Stress itself is not a bad thing. It can often help us perform at our best, expand beyond our limits and achieve things that would otherwise astonish us. Just ask any elite athlete. The real problem lies in the fact that in this age of global anxiety we do not get enough *relief* from stress. So to revitalize yourself and nourish the deepest part of you, plan for a weekly period of peace – a weekly sabbatical – to get back to the simpler pleasures of life, pleasures that you may have given up as your days grew busier and your life more complex. Bringing this simple ritual into your weeks will help you reduce stress, connect with your more creative side and feel far happier in every role of your life.

Your weekly sabbatical does not have to last a full day. All you need are a few hours alone, perhaps on a quiet Sunday morning, when you can spend some time doing the things you love to do the most. Ideas include spending time in your favorite bookstore, watching the sun rise, taking a solitary walk along a beach and writing in your journal. Organizing your life so that you get to do more of the things you love to do is one of the first steps to life improvement. Who cares if others don't understand what you are trying to accomplish by making the weekly sabbatical an essential part of your life. Do it for yourself, you are worth it. In the words of Thoreau, 'If a man does not keep pace with his companions, perhaps it is because he hears a different drummer. Let him step to the music which he hears, however measured or far away.'

11.

Talk to Yourself

<< >>

Years ago, when I was a litigation lawyer who had many of the material trappings of success yet little in the way of inner peace, I read a book called *As a Man Thinketh* by James Allen. The book discussed the enormous power of the human mind to shape our reality and attract great happiness and prosperity into our lives. The work also mentioned the profound influence of the words and language we use on a daily basis to create a more enlightened pathway of thought.

Fascinated, I began to read more and more wisdom and self-help literature. And as I did, I discovered the profound impact and importance of the words we use in our daily communications (both with others and with ourselves) on the quality of our lives. This knowledge also caused me to become aware of the personal dialogue that each of us has going on within us every minute of every hour of every day and to vow to improve the content of what I was saying to myself. To achieve this, I began to apply a strategy developed by the ancient sages over five thousand years ago. And, in many ways, it changed my life.

The technique is a simple one and involves nothing more than selecting a phrase that you will train your mind to focus on at different times throughout the day until it begins to dominate your awareness and reshape the person you are. If it is inner peace and calm you seek, the phrase, known as a mantra, might be, 'I am so grateful that I am a serene and tranquil person.' If it is more confidence that you want, your mantra could be, 'I am delighted that I am full of confidence and boundless courage.' If it is material prosperity you are after, your saying might be, 'I am so grateful that money and opportunity is flowing into my life.'

Repeat your mantras softly under your breath as you walk to work, as you wait in line or as you wash the dishes to fill otherwise unproductive times of your day with a powerful life improvement force. Try to say your personal phrase at least two hundred times a day for at least four weeks. The results will be profound as you take one giant step to finding the peace, prosperity and purpose your life requires. As Hazrat Inayat Khan said, 'The words that enlighten the soul are more precious than jewels.'

12.

SCHEDULE WORRY
BREAKS

〈〈 〓 〉〉

After I wrote *The Monk Who Sold His Ferrari*, I was flooded with letters from readers who saw their lives change from the lessons they discovered on becoming happier, more fulfilled and more peaceful in these stress-crazed times. Many of the letters came from people whose work lives had grown so busy that they spent most of their free time worrying about things that should have been left at the office. They had lost the ability to laugh, love and share joy with their families because challenges at work were consuming them.

Too many people are spending the best years of their lives stuck in a state of constant worry. They worry about their jobs, the bills, the environment and their kids. And yet we all know deep in our hearts that most of the things we worry about never happen. It's like that great saying of Mark Twain's, 'I've had a lot of trouble in my life, some of which actually happened.' My father, a particularly wise man who has had a deep influence on my own life, once told me that the Sanskrit character for funeral pyre is strikingly similar to the Sanskrit character for worry. 'I'm surprised,' I replied. 'You shouldn't be, son,' he gently offered. 'One burns the dead while the other burns the living.'

I know how dramatically the worry habit can reduce one's quality of life from personal experience. While in my late twenties, I was on the so-called fast track to success. I had received two law degrees from one of the country's most prestigious law schools, served as the law clerk for a Chief Justice and was handling highly complex cases as a litigation lawyer. But I was often working too hard and worrying too much. I was waking up on Monday morning with a sinking feeling in the pit of my stomach and a deep sense that I was wasting my talents on work that was not aligned with the person I was. So I began to search for ways to improve my life, turning first to the self-help and life leadership literature, where I found a wealth of lessons for a more balanced, peace-filled and meaningful existence.

One of the simple strategies I learned to conquer the worry habit was to schedule specific times to worry – what I now call 'worry breaks'. If we are facing a difficulty, it is easy to spend all our waking hours focusing on it. Instead, I recommend that you schedule fixed times to worry, say, thirty minutes every evening. During this worry session, you may wallow in your problems and brood over your difficulties. But after that period ends, you must train yourself to leave your troubles behind and do something more productive, such as going for a walk in natural surroundings or reading an inspirational book or having a heart-to-heart conversation with someone you love. If during other times of the day you feel the need to worry, jot down what you want to worry about in a notebook which you can then bring to your next worry break. This simple but powerful technique will help you gradually reduce the amount of time you spend worrying and eventually serve to eliminate this habit forever.

13.

MODEL A CHILD

A while ago, I took my four-year-old son Colby to an Italian restaurant for lunch. It was a beautiful autumn day and, as usual, my young son was full of energy and joy. We both ordered pasta for our main course and then started to enjoy the freshly baked bread our waiter had brought. Little did I know that Colby was about to teach his father yet another lesson in the art of living.

Rather than eating the bread whole as most adults do, Colby took a different, far more creative approach. He began to scoop out the warm, soft part of the bread and left the crust intact. In other words, he had the wisdom to focus on the best part of the bread and leave the rest. Someone once said to me at a seminar, 'Children come to us more highly evolved than adults to teach us the lessons we need to learn.' And on that fine day, my little boy reminded me that as so-called grown-ups, we spend too much time focusing on the 'crust of life' rather than on all the good things that flow in and out of our days. We focus on our challenges at work, the pile of bills we have to pay and the lack of time to do all those things we need to do. But our thoughts do form our world and what we think about does grow in our lives. What we focus on will determine our destiny and so we must start focusing on the good stuff.

In the weeks ahead, make the time to connect to your more playful side, the child within you. Take the time to study the positive qualities of children and model their ability to stay energized, imaginative and completely in the moment no matter what might be going on around them. And as you do, remember the powerful words of Leo Rosten, who observed:

You can understand and relate to most people better if you look at them – no matter how impressive they may be – as if they are children. For most of us never really grow up or mature all that much – we simply grow taller. Oh, to be sure, we laugh less and play less and wear uncomfortable disguises like adults, but beneath the costume is the child we always are, whose needs are simple, whose daily life is still best described by fairy tales.

14.

REMEMBER, GENIUS IS 99 PERCENT INSPIRATION

《‹ ›》

The celebrated inventor Thomas Edison is well known for his statement: 'Genius is 1 percent inspiration and 99 percent perspiration.' While I believe that hard work is essential to a life of real success and fulfillment, I think that being filled with a deep sense of inspiration and commitment to making a difference in the world is an even more important attribute.

All of the great geniuses of the world were inspired and driven by their desire to enrich the lives of others. When you study their lives, you will discover that this desire became almost an obsession for most of them. It consumed them and occupied every cell of their minds. Edison was inspired to manifest the visions he saw on the picture screen of his imagination into reality. Jonas Salk, who discovered the polio vaccine, was inspired to help others from suffering from this dreaded affliction. And Marie Curie, the great Nobel Prize-winning scientist, was inspired to serve humanity through her discovery of radium. As Woodrow Wilson said, 'You are not here to merely make a living. You are here in order to enable the world to live more amply, with greater vision, with a finer spirit of hope and achievement. You are here to enrich the world, and you impoverish yourself if you forget the errand.'

How inspired are you in your own life? Do you jump out of bed on Monday mornings or do you simply lie there with a sense of emptiness flooding through your body? If your level of inspiration is lower than you know it should be, read a good self-help book or listen to a motivating audiocassette program. Attend a public lecture by someone you admire or spend a few hours studying the biography of one of your heroes. Start spending time with people who are passionate about what they are doing in their lives and dedicated to making the best out of life. With a healthy dose of inspiration, you will quickly raise your life to a whole new plane of living.

15.

CARE FOR THE TEMPLE

A few months ago, I had lunch with a colleague in the speaking profession. As we discussed the things we did in our lives to stay focused, balanced and at our peak amid the demands of our busy schedules, he made a powerful point. 'Robin,' he said, 'many people regularly go to a church or temple to stay grounded and centered. I'm a little different. I go to the gym – that's my temple.' He added that no matter how busy he is, at 5:30 p.m. he closes his office and makes the 'daily pilgrimage' to his gym to run a few miles on the treadmill. Nothing can stop him from taking this time to ensure his health and happiness.

My friend's observation made me think of a saying of the ancient Romans that I quoted in my first book *MegaLiving*, 'mens sana in corpore sano,' which is Latin for 'in a sound body rests a sound mind.' It also made me realize that our bodies need to be treated like temples and considered sacred if we hope to live life fully and completely.

Regular exercise will not only improve your health, it will help you think more clearly, boost creativity and manage the relentless stress that seems to dominate our days. And research has proven that exercise will not only add life to your years, it could add years to your life. One study of 18,000 Harvard alumni found that every hour spent on exercise added three hours to the participants' lives. Few investments will yield a better return than time spent on physical fitness. And remember: 'Those who don't make time for exercise must eventually make time for illness.'

In my own life, I have set the goal of swimming five times a week. There is something special about the renewing power of swimming that I cannot begin to describe. I wish I could say I achieve this goal every single week, but I can't. Yet, having such a lofty objective keeps me focused on how important staying in peak physical condition is for my overall well-being and to the quality of my life. Without fail, every workout in the swimming pool brings the same results: I feel energized, serene, balanced and happy. And my exercise sessions also bring me something that I feel is truly priceless: perspective. After my forty-minute swims, any challenges I might be struggling with seem smaller, any worries I have become trivial and I find myself living fully in the present moment. The act of caring for my physical temple reminds me that life's greatest pleasures are often life's simplest ones.

16.

LEARN TO BE SILENT

<< >>

William Wordsworth sagely observed, 'When from our better selves we have too long been parted by the hurrying world, sick of its business, of its pleasures tired, how gracious, how benign is solitude.' When was the last time you made the time to be silent and still? When was the last time you carved out a chunk of time to enjoy the power of solitude to restore, refocus and revitalize your mind, body and spirit?

All of the great wisdom traditions of the world have arrived at the same conclusion: to reconnect with who you really are as a person and to come to know the glory that rests within you, you must find the time to be silent on a regular basis. Sure, you are busy. But as Thoreau said: 'It is not enough to be busy, so are the ants. The question is what are you so busy about?'

The importance of silence makes me think about the story of an old lighthouse keeper. The man had only a limited amount of oil to keep his beacon lit so that passing ships could avoid the rocky shore. One night, a man who lived close by needed to borrow some of this precious commodity to light his home, so the lighthouse keeper gave him some of his own. Another night, a traveler begged for some oil to light his lamp so he could keep on traveling. The lighthouse keeper also complied with this request and gave him the amount he needed. The next night, the lighthouse keeper was awakened by a mother banging on his door. She prayed for some oil so that she could illuminate her home and feed her family. Again he agreed. Soon all his oil was gone and his beacon went out. Many ships ran aground and many lives were lost because the lighthouse keeper forgot to focus on his priority. He neglected his primary duty and paid a high price. Experiencing solitude, for even a few minutes a day, will keep you centered on your highest life priorities and help you avoid the neglect that pervades the lives of so many of us.

And saying that you don't have enough time to be silent on a regular basis is a lot like saying you are too busy driving to stop for gas – eventually it *will* catch up with you.

17.

THINK ABOUT YOUR
IDEAL NEIGHBORHOOD

One of the things I have done along my quest for self-knowledge is to make a list of all the people I wished lived next door to me. These are men and women from both the past and present who I would love to be able to drop in on for a quick cup of tea every once in a while and share a laugh with from time to time. The very act of listing your 'ideal neighbors' will connect you to many of the values and traits you respect the most in people and, in doing so, help you to discover more about yourself as a person. It is also a fun way to spend 30 minutes of your life.

Here are some of the people on my list:

- Norman Vincent Peale, the famed author of *The Power of Positive Thinking*
- Henry David Thoreau, the great American philosopher and the author of *Walden*, one of my favorite books

- Baltasar Gracian, the Jesuit scholar who became one of Spain's greatest writers
- Billie Holiday, the great jazz singer
- Nelson Mandela, the freedom fighter
- Og Mandino, self-help author of such classics as *A Better Way to Live* and *University of Success*
- Mother Teresa, the respected humanitarian
- Richard Branson, the British tycoon and adventurer
- Pierre Elliott Trudeau, the colorful Canadian prime minister
- Miles Davis, the legendary trumpeter
- Muhammad Ali, the world champion boxer
- Benjamin Franklin, the renowned statesman

Take a moment right now to jot down some of the people whom you wished lived on your street. Then think about the qualities that make these men and women so admirable and how you might foster such qualities in your own life. The first step to realizing your life vision is defining it. And the first step to becoming the person you want to be is identifying the traits of the person you want to be.

18.

GET UP EARLY

Getting up early is a gift you give to yourself. Few disciplines have the power to transform your life as does the habit of early rising. There is something very special about the first few hours of the morning. Time seems to slow down and a deep sense of peace fills the air. Joining the 'Five o'Clock Club' will allow you to start controlling your day rather than letting your day control you. Winning the 'Battle of the Bed' and putting 'mind over mattress' by rising early will provide you with at least one quiet hour for yourself during the most crucial part of your day: the beginning. If spent wisely, the rest of your day will unfold in a wonderful way.

In *The Monk Who Sold His Ferrari*, I challenged readers to 'get up with the sun' and offered a number of ideas to help them cultivate this new life discipline. From the many letters, e-mails and faxes I have received from people who have improved the quality of their lives by getting up at 5 a.m., I can safely say that this is one success principle that is really worth integrating into your life. In doing so, you will join the ranks of many of the most influential people of our time ranging from Mahatma Gandhi, Thomas Edison and Nelson Mandela to Ted Turner and Mary Kay Ash.

One reader of *The Monk*, a marketing executive, wrote that her stress level fell so dramatically once she started rising early that her team at the office presented her with a paperweight bearing the following inscription: 'To our MIP (Most Improved Player). Whatever you are doing, keep doing it. You are an inspiration to us all.' A consummate late riser, she vowed to stop sleeping in and spending her days making up for time lost while under the blanket. So while her family (and the world around her) slept, she began to get up first at 6 a.m., then at 5:30 a.m. and finally at 5 a.m. During the free time that she found she had created, she would do all the things she loved to do but had somehow never found time for. Listening carefully to classical music, writing letters, reading the classics and walking were just some of the activities that she used to rekindle her spirit and reconnect with a part of herself she thought she had lost. By getting up early, she began to care for herself again. And by doing so, she became a much better parent, spouse and professional.

To cultivate the habit of getting up earlier, the first thing to remember is that it is the quality rather than the quantity of sleep that matters most. It is better to have six hours of uninterrupted sleep than ten hours of restless, broken sleep. Here are four tips to help you sleep more deeply:

- Don't rehearse the activities of your day while you are lying in bed trying to get to sleep.
- Don't eat after 8 p.m. (If you have to eat something, have soup.)
- Don't watch the news before you go to sleep.
- Don't read in bed.

Give yourself a few weeks for this new habit to take hold. Saying that you tried to get up early but gave up after seven days because it was just too hard is like saying you tried taking French lessons for a week but gave up because you could not speak the language by then. Life change takes time, effort and patience. But the results you will receive make the initial stress you experience more than worth it.

19.

SEE YOUR TROUBLES
AS BLESSINGS

During the life leadership seminars I give, I often ask the participants this question: 'Who would agree with me that we learn the most from our most difficult experiences?' Inevitably, nearly every hand in the room goes up. Given this, I often wonder why we, as human beings, spend so much of our lives focusing on the negative aspects of our most difficult experiences rather than seeing them for what they truly are: our greatest teachers.

You would not have the wisdom and knowledge you now possess were it not for the setbacks you have faced, the mistakes you have made and the suffering you have endured. Once and for all, come to realize that pain is a teacher and failure is the highway to success. You cannot learn how to play the guitar without hitting a few wrong notes and you will never learn how to sail if you are not willing to tip the boat over a few times. Begin to see your troubles as blessings, resolve to transform your stumbling blocks into stepping stones and vow to turn your wounds into wisdom.

Like most people, I have encountered my own share of pain as I have advanced along the path of life. But I always try to remind myself that our character is shaped, not through life's easiest experiences, but during life's toughest ones. It is during life's most trying times that we discover who we really are and the fullness of the strength that lies within us. If you are currently experiencing challenges of your own, I respectfully offer the following words of Rainer Maria Rilke, which have helped me greatly when life throws one of its curves my way:

> ... have patience with everything that remains unsolved in your heart. Try to love the questions themselves, like locked rooms and like books written in a foreign language. Do not now look for the answers. They cannot now be given to you because you could not live them. It is a question of experiencing everything. At present, you need to live the question. Perhaps you will gradually, without even noticing it, find yourself experiencing the answer, some distant day.

20.

LAUGH MORE

According to one study, the average four-year-old laughs three hundred times a day while the average adult laughs about fifteen times a day. With all the obligations, stresses and activities that fill our days, we have forgotten how to laugh. Daily laughter has been shown to elevate our moods, promote creativity and give us more energy. Comedian Steve Martin reportedly laughs for five minutes in front of the mirror every morning to get his creative juices flowing and to start his day on a high note (try it – it works). Laughter therapy has even been used to cure illnesses and heal those with serious ailments. As William James, the father of modern psychology, observed, 'We don't laugh because we are happy. We are happy because we laugh.'

A friend of mine, always known for his wise ways, made it his new year's resolution one year to laugh more. Every few weeks, he would go to his local video store and rent a Three Stooges movie or buy a new book of humor, which he would then dip into when he had a few free moments during the course of his day. A positive person already, he began to notice that he felt even happier and started to laugh even more than before he undertook this personal development initiative. Because of all the humor he surrounded himself with and the new awareness it created in his life, he also began to see the lighter side of things and no longer experienced the level of stress he had felt in his professional pursuits. This simple discipline raised him to a whole new level of living and effectiveness.

Why not follow my friend's lead and head down to your local video store to stock up on the latest funny movies? Then pick up a few books, perhaps something from Gary Larson's Far Side series or the much-read Dilbert cartoons, to stimulate your laughter habit. Reconnect to your playful side and enjoy the wonders of a deep belly laugh.

21.

SPEND A DAY
WITHOUT YOUR WATCH

〈〈 ᐧ 〉〉

Last fall, I did something I have not done for many years: I left my watch at home and spent an entire day without looking at the time. Rather than living by the clock and planning everything I was going to do that day, I simply lived for the moment and did whatever I felt like doing. I became a true human *being* rather than merely a human doing.

Early in the morning, I went for a walk deep in the woods, one of my favorite things to do. With me, I carried an old paperback copy of *Walden* by the social philosopher Henry David Thoreau, a book I have come to love. After finding a beautiful place to sit and read, I experienced one of those moments of synchronicity where something perfect happens at just the right time. For me it was randomly opening the book and finding the following paragraph in front of me:

I went to the woods because I wished to live deliberately, to front only the essential facts of life, and see if I could not learn what it had to teach, and not, when I came to die, discover that I had not lived. I did not wish to live what was not life, living is so dear; nor did I wish to practice resignation, unless it was quite necessary. I wanted to live deep and suck out all the marrow of life, to live so sturdily and Spartan-like as to put to rout all that was not life ...

I reflected on this great man's words and soaked up the miraculous beauty of the scene around me. The rest of the day was spent in a bookshop, watching *Toy Story* with my kids, relaxing with the family on our patio and listening to my favorite pieces of music. Nothing expensive. Nothing complicated. But completely fun.

22.

TAKE MORE RISKS

$\ll \gg$

I'll make you this promise: on your deathbed, in the twilight of your life, it will not be all the risks you took that you will regret the most. Rather, what will fill your heart with the greatest amount of regret and sadness will be all those risks that you did not take, all those opportunities you did not seize and all those fears you did not face. Remember that on the other side of fear lies freedom. And stay focused on the timeless success principle that says: 'life is nothing more that a game of numbers – the more risks you take, the more rewards you will receive.' Or in the words of Sophocles, 'Fortune is not on the side of the faint-hearted.'

To live your life to the fullest, start taking more risks and doing the things you fear. Get good at being uncomfortable and stop walking the path of least resistance. Sure, there is a greater chance you will stub your toes when you walk the road less traveled, but that is the only way you can get anywhere. As my wise mother always says, 'you cannot get to third base with one foot on second.' Or as André Gide observed, 'One does not discover new lands without consenting to lose sight of the shore for a very long time.'

The real secret to a life of abundance is to stop spending your days searching for security and to start spending your time pursuing opportunity. Sure, you will meet with your share of failures if you start living more deliberately and passionately. But failure is nothing more than learning how to win. Or as my dad observed one day, 'Robin, it's risky out on a limb. But that's where all the fruit is.'

As I wrote in an earlier lesson, life is all about choices. Deeply fulfilled and highly actualized people simply make wiser choices than others. You can choose to spend the rest of your days sitting on the shore of life in complete safety or you can take some chances, dive deep into the water and discover the pearls that lie waiting for the person of true courage. To keep me inspired and centered on the fact that I must keep stretching my own personal boundaries as the days go by, I have posted the following words of Theodore Roosevelt in the study where I write:

It is not the critic who counts, not the man who points out how the strong man stumbled, or where the doer of deeds could have done better. The credit belongs to the man who is actually in the arena, whose face is marred by dust and sweat and blood, who strives valiantly, who errs and comes short again and again, who knows the great enthusiasms, the great devotions, and spends himself in a worthy cause, who at best knows in the end the triumphs of high achievement and who at the worst, if he fails, at least fails while daring greatly so that his place shall never be with those cold and timid souls who know neither victory nor defeat.

23.

LIVE A LIFE

On being asked about the ups and downs of his career, movie star Kevin Costner responded with these words, 'I'm living a life.' I found this reply to be profound. Rather than spending his days judging the events and experiences of his life as either good or bad, he adopted a neutral stance and simply decided to accept them for what they are: a natural part of the path he is on.

We all travel different roads to our ultimate destinations. For some of us, the path is rockier than for others. But no one reaches the end without facing some form of adversity. So rather than fight it, why not accept it as the way of life? Why not detach yourself from the outcomes and simply experience every circumstance that enters your life to the fullest? Feel the pain and savor the happiness. If you have never visited the valleys, the view from the mountaintop is not as breathtaking. Remember, there are no real failures in life, only results. There are no true tragedies, only lessons. And there really are no problems, only opportunities waiting to be recognized as solutions by the person of wisdom.

24.

LEARN FROM A
GOOD MOVIE

<< >>

I love going to the movies whenever I can. Often, I take my young daughter Bianca and my son Colby with me and, while munching on popcorn, we enjoy the latest animated film that is heating up the box office. We always walk out with smiles on our faces along with a whole host of new characters we can pretend to be in our daily play sessions. When I am on the road for a speaking tour, I still try to find a few hours at the end of the day to slip into a theater in whatever city I may be in and watch a good movie. I find that films not only relax me but they serve to transport me to a different world and inspire me to keep thinking about the endless possibilities life holds. I guess movies bring out the dreamer in me.

Recently, I saw an Italian movie called *Life Is Beautiful*. Though it was subtitled, it kept me riveted for nearly three hours and moved me like no film I have seen in quite some time. Much of the story centers on a loving father and his relationship with his young son. Early on, the two are inseparable and share many great times. Suddenly, one afternoon, the two are taken away from their home and placed on a train bound for Auschwitz, the notorious Nazi concentration camp. The rest of the movie shows the incredible lengths the father goes to, not only to keep his son alive, but to actually keep him happy through their horrifying ordeal. Though the father ultimately sacrifices his own life at the end, *Life Is Beautiful* is a powerful reminder that living is a gift and we must make the best of it, every day of our lives.

A good movie can restore your perspective, reconnect you to the things you value most and keep you enthusiastic about all the things in your life. And as Ralph Waldo Emerson said, 'Nothing great was ever achieved without enthusiasm.'

25.

BLESS YOUR MONEY

If you ever get to London, England, visit Foyle's, which is among the oldest bookstores in the city. I have found more gems by browsing along its dusty shelves than in any other bookshop I have visited around the world. Being a dedicated student of self-help literature myself, I generally gravitate to that section in the store. I always look for a little-known work that will offer me a few new insights on the art of living and help me improve the quality of my own life. And in Foyle's, I always find one.

A few years back, I found a book entitled *Bring Out the Magic in Your Mind*. It was written almost thirty years ago by a man named Al Koran, who was then known as 'the Finest Mental Magician in the World'. In a chapter entitled 'The Secret of Wealth' he writes the following: 'When you send your money out, remember always to bless it. Ask it to bless everybody that it touches, and command it to go out and feed the hungry and clothe the naked, and command it to come back to you a millionfold. Don't pass over this lightly. I am serious.'

Over the next few days, why not follow Al Koran's advice and see what happens? When you pay for your groceries, silently bless all those who have helped bring this food to you: the farmers who have grown it, the delivery people who have carried it and the store clerks who have stocked it. If you are writing a check for your children's education, why not give silent appreciation to all the teachers who are spending their days shaping the minds of your kids and to all the others who make their work possible? When you pull out a few bills to buy that magazine off the rack in a convenience store, bless the person who is toiling away behind the counter and hope the money adds value to the quality of his or her life. As that timeless truth says, 'The hand that gives is the hand that gathers.'

26.

FOCUS ON THE WORTHY

A while ago a FedEx package arrived at my office. Inside was an envelope with a gold seal placed on the fold and my name carefully written on the front. I quickly opened it and began to read the letter within. It was from the CEO of a major corporation who had picked up my book *Leadership Wisdom from the Monk Who Sold His Ferrari* at an airport while on his way to a business meeting in Europe. He said he was a lifelong student of leadership and was intrigued by the title, which had brought a smile to his face.

This executive had been under tremendous pressure as a result of the overwhelming demands placed on him and was hoping to learn some ways to improve his leadership effectiveness so that he could spend more time on the things that really mattered, both in his business life and in his personal world. In his letter, he wrote:

As I read your story about this man whose life had become too complex and out of control, I began to connect with a part of myself that I had not connected with for many, many years. I began to think about the people in my organization who look to me for guidance and inspiration. I began to think about my wife who had been begging me to take a vacation for the past five years. And I thought about my three children who had watched their father spend the finest years of their youth climbing the imaginary ladder of success. I consider myself a strong person but as I continued to read your book, I began to sob, quietly at first and then uncontrollably, so much so that the flight attendant rushed over and politely asked if everything was alright.

The CEO continued:

That moment was a wake-up call for me, an experience I will carry with me until the day that I die. I knew that I had to make some serious changes in the way that I was leading and in the way that I was living. So on that flight, sitting 35,000 feet above the world below, I promised myself that I would commit myself to eliminating the multitude of distractions in my life and concentrate on only the fundamentals, those few activities that really had the power to make a difference in the way I worked and lived. I promised to stop reading six newspapers a day, handling every piece of mail that appeared in my in-basket and accepting every dinner invitation that came my way. I even had the title of your chapter on personal effectiveness, which you aptly called 'Focus on the Worthy', made into a plaque that I keep on my desk to remind me that 'the person who tries to do everything ultimately achieves nothing.' I cannot tell you how much better my life has become since I began to live by this simple philosophy. Thank you.

Time is your most precious commodity and yet most of us live our lives as if we have all the time in the world. The real secret to getting control of your life is to restore a sense of focus in your days. The real secret to getting things done is knowing what things need to be left undone. Once you start spending the hours of your days only on those high-leverage activities and priorities that will advance your life's mission and legacy, everything will change. Many of history's greatest thinkers have arrived at the same conclusion. The sage Confucius put it this way, 'The person who chases two rabbits catches neither,' while the Roman philosopher Marcus Aurelius said, 'Let thine occupations be few if thou wouldst lead a tranquil life.' Management guru Peter Drucker made the point of wisdom in yet another way when he wrote, 'There is nothing so useless as doing efficiently that which should not be done at all.'

27.

WRITE THANK-YOU NOTES

<< >>

The things that are easy to do are also the things that are easy not to do. The more the pace of our lives speeds up, the greater the impact the simple gestures of life will have on those most deserving of them. And near the very top of my list of simple gestures that have profound consequences is the lost art of writing thank-you notes.

Everyone loves getting mail – it's a fact of human nature. We all have a deep-seated need to feel important. I truly love receiving letters from people who have read my books and used the lessons within them to make positive changes in their lives. Few things excite me as much as receiving a bag full of mail from men and women who have attended one of my seminars and seen their careers take off and their personal lives improve. And knowing how much joy I feel when I receive mail from others, I try my best to respond to every letter that comes across my desk with a thank-you note of my own.

Even in the case of the people I deal with on a daily basis – executives calling to book me for a speaking engagement, people who attend my personal coaching programs, members of the media requesting an interview and businesspeople calling me with new opportunities – I try to follow up on every encounter with a sincerely written thank-you note. Sure, it takes time. Sure, there might be pressing things on my agenda. But few acts have the power to build and cement relationships like a heartfelt letter of thanks. It shows you care and that you are considerate and human. So this week, go out and buy a package of the blank thank-you cards that are now available in bulk at your local office supply warehouse and start writing. You – and all the people that you deal with – will be glad you did.

28.

ALWAYS CARRY A
BOOK WITH YOU

$\left(\left\langle\ ~\right\rangle\right)$

According to *U.S. News & World Report*, over the course of your lifetime, you will spend eight months opening junk mail, two years unsuccessfully returning phone calls and five years standing in line. Given this startling fact, one of the simplest yet smartest time management strategies you can follow is to never go anywhere without a book under your arm. While others waiting in line are complaining, you will be growing and feeding your mind a rich diet of ideas found in great books.

'So long as you live, keep learning how to live,' noted the Roman philosopher Seneca. Yet most people never read more than a handful of books after they complete their formal schooling. In these times of rapid change, ideas are the commodity of success. All it takes is one idea from the right book to reshape your character or to transform your relationships or to revolutionize your life. A good book can change the way you live as the philosopher Henry David

Thoreau observed in *Walden*, 'There are probably words addressed to our condition exactly, which, if we could really hear and understand, would be more salutary than the morning or the spring to our lives, and possibly put a new aspect on the face of things for us. How many a man has dated a new era of his life from the reading of a book. The book exists for us perchance which will explain our miracles and reveal new ones.'

How high you will rise in your life will be determined not by how hard you work but by how well you think. As I say in my leadership speeches, 'The greatest leaders in this new economy will be the greatest thinkers.' And the person you will be five years from now will come down to two primary influences: the people you associate with and the books you read. I often joke with my seminar audiences that I play 'Cinderella Tennis': I try hard but I never quite make it to the ball. Yet when I play tennis with someone better than I am, something almost magical happens to my game. I make shots that I have never made before, gracefully floating through the air with an ease that would make even the best player blush. Reading good books creates much the same phenomenon. When you expose your mind to the thoughts of the greatest people who have walked this planet before you, your game improves, the depth of your thinking expands and you rise to a whole new level of wisdom.

Deep reading allows you to connect with the world's most creative, intelligent and inspiring people, twenty-four hours a day. Aristotle, Emerson, Seneca, Gandhi, Thoreau, Dorothea Brande, and many of the wisest women and men who grace our planet today are just waiting to share their knowledge with you through their books. Why wouldn't you seize such an opportunity as often as you could? If you have not read today, you have not really lived today. And knowing how to read but failing to do so puts you in exactly the same position as the person who cannot read but wants to.

29.

CREATE A LOVE ACCOUNT

Mother Teresa once said, 'There are no great acts. There are only small acts done with great love.' What small acts can you do today to deepen the bonds between you and the people you value the most? What random acts of kindness and senseless acts of beauty can you offer to someone in an effort to make his or her day just a little better? The irony of being more compassionate is that the very act of giving to others makes you feel better as well.

To practice being more loving, create a love account. Each day, make a few deposits in this very special reserve by doing something small to add joy to the life of someone around you. Buying your partner fresh cut flowers for no reason at all, sending your best friend a copy of your favorite book or taking the time to tell your children in no uncertain terms how you feel about them are all good places to start.

If there is one thing that I have learned in life, it is that the little things are the big things. Those tiny, daily deposits into the love account will give you far more happiness than any amount of money in your bank account. As Emerson said so eloquently, 'Without the rich heart, wealth is an ugly beggar.' Or as Tolstoy wrote, 'The means to gain happiness is to throw out for oneself like a spider in all directions an adhesive web of love, and to catch in all that comes.'

30.

GET BEHIND
PEOPLE'S EYEBALLS

<< >>

One of the deepest of all the human hungers is the need to be understood, cherished and honored. Yet, in the fast-paced days we live in, too many people believe that listening involves nothing more than waiting for the other person to stop talking. And to make matters worse, while that person is speaking, we are all too often using that time to formulate our own response, rather than empathizing with the point being made.

Taking the time to truly understand another's point of view shows that you value what he has to say and care about him as a person. When you start 'getting behind the eyeballs' of the person who is speaking and try to see the world from his perspective, you will connect with him deeply and build high-trust relationships that last.

We have two ears and one mouth for a reason: to listen twice as much as we speak. And having the courtesy to be a better listener has another advantage: since you are not doing all the talking, you are doing all the learning, gaining access to information you would have missed had you been engaged in the usual monologue.

Here are a few practical tips to become better at the art of listening:

- If you are speaking and the person you are having a conversation with has not said something within the past sixty seconds, there is a good chance you have lost her and it's time to stop talking so much.
- Resist the temptation to interrupt. Catch yourself just before you do so and pay more attention to the content of what the other person is saying to you.
- If appropriate (i.e., in a business setting), take notes. Few things more readily show the other person in a conversation that you genuinely wish to learn from what she has to say than pulling out a notepad and making notes while she speaks.
- After the other person makes her points, rather than immediately responding with your opinion, reflect on what you have just heard. Saying something such as, 'Just to make sure I understand you, are you saying …?' and doing so with complete sincerity will bring you much closer to the people you interact with every day of your life.

31.

LIST YOUR PROBLEMS

'A problem well stated is a problem half solved,' said Charles Kettering. There is something very special that happens when you take out a piece of paper and list every single one of your problems on it. It is very much like the peaceful feeling you get after telling your best friend about something that has been troubling you for weeks. A weight somehow falls from your shoulders. You feel lighter, calmer and freer.

I have discovered that while our minds can be our best friends, they can also be our worst enemies. If you keep thinking about your problems, pretty soon you will find you think about little else. The mind is a strange creature in this regard: the things you want it to remember it forgets, but all those things you want it to forget, it remembers. I have people coming to my seminars who tell me they are still mad about what someone did to them fifteen years ago or still annoyed at what a rude salesclerk said to them last month.

To let go of the mental clutter that your problems tend to generate, list all your worries on a piece of paper. If you do so, they will no longer be able to fester in your mind and drain your valuable energy. This simple exercise will also permit you to put your problems into perspective and tackle them in an orderly, well-planned sequence. Among the many successful people who have used this technique are martial arts master Bruce Lee and Winston Churchill, who once said, 'It helps to write down half a dozen things which are worrying me. Two of them, say, disappear; about two, nothing can be done, so it's no use worrying; and two perhaps can be settled.'

32.

PRACTICE THE
ACTION HABIT

〈〈 ‿ 〉〉

'Wisdom is knowing what to do next, skill is knowing how to do it, and virtue is doing it,' observed David Starr Jordan. Most of us know what we need to do in order to live happier, healthier and more fulfilling lives. The real problem is that we don't do what we know. I have heard many motivational speakers say, 'Knowledge is power.' I disagree. Knowledge is not power. Knowledge is only *potential* power. It transforms itself into actual power the moment you decisively act on it.

The mark of a strong character lies not in doing what is fun to do or what is easy to do. The sign of deep moral authority appears in the individual who consistently does what he *ought* to be doing rather than what he *feels* like doing. A person of true character spends his days doing that which is the right thing to do. Rather than watching television for three hours after an exhausting day at work, he has the courage to get up off the couch and read to his kids. Instead of sleeping in on those cold wintry mornings, this individual exercises his natural reserves of self-discipline and gets out of bed for a run. And since action is a habit, the more positive actions you take, the more you will feel like taking.

All too often, we spend our days waiting for the ideal path to appear in front of us. We forget that paths are made by walking, not waiting. Dreaming is great. But thinking big thoughts alone will not build a business, pay your bills or make you into the person you know in your heart you can be. In the words of Thomas Carlyle, 'The end of man is an action and not a thought, though it were the noblest.' The smallest of actions is always better than the boldest of intentions.

33.

SEE YOUR CHILDREN
AS GIFTS

∽∽∽

On Father's Day, my son Colby brought home a handmade
card from school. On the front of it was his small hand-
print and inside the card, above a little photograph of my
child, were these words:

> *Sometimes you get discouraged because I am so*
> *   small*
> *And always leave my fingerprints on furniture and*
> *   walls.*
> *But every day I'm growing – I'll be grown up*
> *   someday*
> *And all those tiny handprints will surely fade away.*
>
> *So here's a final handprint, just so you can recall*
> *Exactly how my fingers looked, when I was very*
> *   small.*
> *Love, Colby*

Children grow so very quickly. It seems like just yesterday that I stood in the delivery room waiting for the birth of my son, and then two years later, for the birth of my daughter, Bianca. It is easy to promise yourself you will spend more time with your kids 'when things slow down at work' or 'when I get that big promotion' or 'next year when I get a little more time'. But if you don't act on life, life has a habit of acting on you. The weeks slip into months, the months slip into years and before you know it, that little child is now an adult with a family of her own. The greatest gift you can give to your children is the gift of your time. And one of the greatest gifts you will ever give yourself is that of enjoying your kids and seeing them for what they truly are: the small miracles of life.

In *The Prophet*, Kahlil Gibran makes the point far more eloquently than I ever could when he writes, 'Your children are not your children. They are the sons and daughters of Life's longing for itself.'

34.

ENJOY THE PATH,
NOT JUST THE REWARD

In my work, I am often asked to teach people how to set and achieve goals. When I ask my audiences, 'Why is it so important that you realize your goals?' they often answer, 'Because getting the things I want will make me happy.' While there is an element of truth in this answer – getting the things we want often does bring a measure of joy into our lives – it somehow misses the mark. The real value of setting and achieving goals lies not in the rewards you receive *but in the person you become* as a result of reaching your goals. This simple distinction has helped me to enjoy the path of life while, at the same time, staying focused on meeting my personal and professional objectives.

As one of my favorite philosophers, Ralph Waldo Emerson, observed, 'The reward for a thing well done, is to have done it.' When you achieve a goal, whether that goal was to be a wiser leader or to become a better parent, you will have grown as a person in the process. Often, you will not be able to detect this growth, but the growth will have occurred. So rather than savoring only the rewards that have flowed from the achievement of that goal, celebrate the fact that the process of reaching your destination has improved the person you are. You have built self-discipline, discovered new things about your abilities and manifested more of your human potential. These are reward in and of themselves.

35.

REMEMBER THAT
AWARENESS PRECEDES
CHANGE

You will never be able to eliminate a weakness you don't even know about. The first step to eliminating a negative habit is to become aware of it. Once you develop an awareness about the behavior you are trying to change, you will be well on your way to replacing it with one that is more helpful.

As an author, I am frequently invited to appear on radio and television talk shows. When I first started doing these programs, I thought I was a natural. I enjoyed meeting the hosts, sharing my insights and discussing the ideas in my books with callers. It was only when I began to tape myself and study those tapes that I realized something I had been unaware of: I spoke far too quickly. As a matter of fact, I sometimes spoke so fast that many of the key points I was trying to make got lost in the avalanche of words I heaped on the audience that had tuned in. Becoming aware of my weakness was the first step to eliminating it.

I then went to my favorite bookstore and bought five books on effective communication. In addition I ordered a series of audiocassettes that contained the speeches of some of the world's top speakers. I also joined the National Speakers Association. Finally, I picked up the phone and called a number of media personalities whom I felt I could learn from and invited them out for a quick lunch. Not one refused. Over a matter of weeks, I educated myself on how to improve my delivery on TV and radio so that I could share my message more effectively.

I have found as well that becoming aware of a weakness, that is, paying attention to it, also attracts more solutions into one's life. For example, as soon as I realized that I needed to slow down to communicate in a better way, I started to notice seminars on the subject advertised in the paper. I also noticed that the right books appeared on the shelves of the bookstores where I was browsing and found people who could coach me. So, over the coming weeks, reflect on your weaknesses and vow to transform them into strengths that will add richness and energy to the way you live.

36.

READ *TUESDAYS* WITH *MORRIE*

∞ $\gg$

While I was on the Denver stop of the American book tour for *The Monk Who Sold His Ferrari*, I dropped into the airport bookstore before boarding the flight home. As I looked through the latest bestsellers, a small book with a simple cover caught my attention. Its title read *Tuesdays with Morrie: An Old Man, a Young Man and Life's Greatest Lesson*. This was the book that at least a dozen booksellers on the tour had suggested I buy since it was, in many ways, similar to the one I had just written. And so I picked it up.

After takeoff, I thought I would browse through the book for a few minutes before taking a much-needed nap. A few minutes slipped into a few hours and by the time we landed, I had just finished the last page with tears in my eyes. The book is about a man who, after leaving university and building a career, rediscovers his favorite professor, Morrie, in the final months of the older man's life. Every Tuesday, the former student then visits the dying teacher to learn another lesson about life from this man who has lived so richly and completely.

A real-life account, the lessons Morrie offers during these moving Tuesday sessions include: how to avoid a life of regret, the value of family, the importance of forgiveness and the meaning of death, where he makes the powerful remark, 'Once you learn how to die, you learn how to live.' This beautiful little book will remind you of the importance of counting your blessings daily and having the wisdom to honor life's simplest pleasures no matter how busy your life becomes. One of the legacies I will leave to my two children will be a library of books that have inspired and touched me. And *Tuesdays with Morrie* will be one that will sit out in front.

37.

MASTER YOUR TIME

〈〈 ᐟᐟ 〉〉

I have always found it ironic that so many people say they would do anything for a little more time every day and yet they squander the time they already have. Time is life's great leveler. We all have the same allotment of twenty-four hours in a day. What separates the people who create great lives from the also-rans is how they use these hours.

Most of us live as if we have an infinite amount of time to do all the things we know we must do to live a full and rewarding life. And so we procrastinate and put the achievement of our dreams on hold while we tend to those daily emergencies that fill up our days. This is a certain recipe for a life of regret. As novelist Paul Bowles once wrote:

... because we don't know [when we will die], we get to think of life as an inexhaustible well. Yet everything happens only a certain number of times, and a very small number, really. How many more times will you remember a certain afternoon of your childhood, some afternoon that's so deeply a part of your being that you can't even conceive of your life without it? Perhaps four or five times more. Perhaps not even that. How many more times will you watch the full moon rise? Perhaps twenty. And yet it all seems limitless.

Commit yourself to managing your time more effectively. Develop a keen sense of awareness about how important your time really is. Don't let people waste this most precious of commodities and invest it only in those activities that truly count.

38.

KEEP YOUR COOL

≪ ≫

'Anyone can become angry – that's easy. But to be angry with the right person, to the right degree, at the right time, for the right purpose, and in the right way – that is not easy,' taught Aristotle. With all the stress and pressure in our lives, it is easy to lose our cool at the slightest irritation. While we are rushing home from work at the end of another exhausting day, we scream at the slow driver in front of us who apparently has all the time in the world. While we shop at the grocery store, we get annoyed with the stock clerk who sends us to the wrong aisle when we are in search of the ingredients for tonight's lasagna. And while we are eating our dinner, we yell at the telemarketer who has the nerve to interrupt us in an attempt to sell us their latest wares.

The problem with losing your temper on a daily basis is that it becomes a habit. And like most habits, a time arrives when it becomes second nature. Personal-relationships start unraveling, business partnerships begin to fall apart and your credibility decreases as you become known as 'a loose cannon'. Effective people are consistent and, in many ways, predictable. Tough times call for cool people and they are always cool and calm when the pressure is on. Keeping your cool in a moment of crisis can save you years of pain and anguish. Hurtful words unleashed in a single minute of anger have led to many a broken friendship. Words are like arrows: once released, they are impossible to retrieve. So choose yours with care.

An excellent way to control your temper is simply to count to 100 before you respond to someone who has irritated you. Another strategy to use is what I call the 'Three Gate Test'. The ancient sages would only speak if the words they were about to utter passed three gates. At the first gate, they asked themselves, Are these words truthful? If so, the words could then pass on to the second gate. At the second gate, the sages asked, Are these words necessary? If so, they would then pass on to the third gate, where they would ask, Are these words kind? If so, then only would they leave their lips and be sent out into the world. 'Treat people as if they were what they ought to be and help them become what they are capable of being,' said the German poet Johann Wolfgang von Goethe. These are wise words to live by.

39.

RECRUIT A BOARD
OF DIRECTORS

To succeed in these times of breakneck change, companies will often recruit a board of directors to help them make more effective decisions and lead them in the right direction during stormy times. By consulting men and women of wisdom these organizations reduce the number of mistakes they make, boost corporate effectiveness and increase their credibility in the marketplace.

One client of mine has a different approach to the concept of having a board of directors. A seasoned entrepreneur and a participant in one of the monthly life coaching programs I conduct across the country, this woman told me that during her periods of silent contemplation, she sits in a room with a pen and pad of paper and writes down a problem that she is facing. Sometimes it involves a difficulty in a relationship, sometimes it concerns a money issue or at other times a struggle that is more spiritual in nature.

Once in a state of deep relaxation, she then calls upon her personal board of directors to help her solve problems. The twist? The members of her board are no longer alive. In her imagination, she seeks the wise counsel of many of history's greatest thinkers. When confronting a problem that requires a creative solution, she asks Leonardo da Vinci, 'How might you deal with this?' On facing a challenge that requires her to have more courage, she asks aviation pioneer Amelia Earhart, 'What would you do in this situation?' And when the issue involves money, she asks the late billionaire Sam Walton, widely known for his common sense, 'Sam, how would you handle this?' This technique has truly worked wonders for her, improved her creative thinking ability and kept her peaceful during turbulent times.

Who would you invite to sit on your imaginary board of directors? Here are some of the people I'd love to have on my council:

- Ben Franklin for guidance on issues involving character
- Albert Schweitzer to remind me of the importance of service to others
- Mahatma Gandhi and Nelson Mandela for leadership issues
- Bruce Lee for advice on self-discipline
- Marie Curie for questions relating to innovation
- Viktor Frankl, famed holocaust survivor, for guidance about how to deal with adversity

40.

CURE YOUR
MONKEY MIND

$\ll \gg$

To get the best from life, you must be completely present and mindful in every minute of every hour of every day. As Albert Camus wrote, 'Real generosity towards the future consists in giving all to what is present.' Yet, on most days, our minds are in ten different places at any one time. Rather than enjoying the walk to work, we wonder what the boss will say to us when we get to the office or what we will have for lunch or how our children will do at school today. Our minds are like scampering puppies or, as they say in the East, like unchained monkeys, rushing from place to place without any pause for peace.

By developing present moment awareness and an abundance of mental focus, you will not only feel much calmer in your life, you will also unlock the fullness of your mind's potential. When too many distractions compete for your attention, the power of your mind is dissipated in all those different directions rather than concentrated on one point like the rays of a laser beam. The good news is that you can practice becoming more attentive to the present and develop this skill within a relatively short period of time.

One of the best ways to cure your monkey mind is through a technique I call 'Focused Reading'. Every time your mind wanders from the page into a daydream or a worry, make a checkmark in the righthand margin of the page. This simple act will increase your awareness of how poorly you concentrate and, since awareness is the first step to change, help you to build the skills you need for a clearer, quieter mind.

41.

GET GOOD AT ASKING

〔 〕

'He who asks may be a fool for five minutes. He who doesn't is a fool for a lifetime,' goes the wise Chinese proverb. It makes me think of an ad I read in the classifieds recently that said, 'To the beautiful woman in the brown suede coat at the drugstore at [street location provided] on Saturday, November 28 @ 4 p.m. You bumped into me in front of the magazine section. I would love to meet and chat.' The man who placed this ad then left his phone number. Destiny had given him an opportunity – possibly to meet the woman of his dreams – and he had squandered it. And now, after regretting the fact that he 'did not ask', he has had to resort to placing an ad in the newspaper in the desperate hope of finding this woman.

The more you ask, the more you get, but it takes practice to get good at it. Success is a numbers game. As the Buddhist sages observed, 'Every arrow that hits the bull's eye is the result of one hundred misses.' Over the coming weeks, flex your 'asking muscles' by asking for a better table at your favorite restaurant, for a free second scoop at your local ice cream shop or for a complimentary upgrade on your next airline flight. You might be surprised at the abundance that will flow into your life when you just ask sincerely for the things you want. Remember, the person who asks for what he wants at least has a chance of getting what he wants. The person who does not ask has no chance. One of the best books I have read on the power of asking is *The Aladdin Factor*, written by my friend and speaking colleague Mark Victor Hansen along with self-esteem expert Jack Canfield. Full of practical ideas and simple techniques, the book also contains a wealth of inspiring quotes like this one from Somerset Maugham: 'It's a funny thing about life; if you refuse to accept anything but the best, you very often get it.'

42.

LOOK FOR THE HIGHER
MEANING OF YOUR WORK

<< >>

One of my favorite magazines is *Fast Company*. It provides a refreshingly human look at the new world of work. In a recent issue, Xerox PARC guru John Seely Brown said something that really made me think: 'The job of leadership today is not just to make money, it's to make meaning.'

In the old days, most of us were content to have a job that simply paid the bills. But now, we crave so much more in our work. We want fulfillment, creative challenge, growth, joy and a sense that we are living for something more than ourselves. In a word, we seek meaning. One of the best ways to find the higher meaning in the work you do is to use the technique of creative questioning to become aware of the impact your work has on the world around you. Ask yourself questions like, Who ultimately benefits from the products and services my company offers? or What difference do my daily efforts make? Once you do so, you will start noticing the connection between the work you do and the lives you touch.

For example, if you are a teacher, stop focusing on all the tremendous changes in your profession, and remember that every day you enter that classroom, you have the privilege to shape a young mind. There are children and families that count on you. If you are a financial adviser, remain centered on the fact that your services help people retire early, build the homes they have always wanted and fulfill their dreams. If you are an insurance professional, remember that you help people bring security to their lives and serve them in times of need. And if you are a retail clerk, think about how your work serves people and how the products you offer them add joy to their lives.

By concentrating on the value your work adds and the contribution you make, you will see quantum improvements in your satisfaction and motivation levels. Few things energize the human spirit more than the desire to make a difference in the lives of others. Mahatma Gandhi knew this. Nelson Mandela knew this. And Mother Teresa knew this. The simple shift of mind I am encouraging you to make can bring a whole new sense of enjoyment into your life.

43.

BUILD A LIBRARY
OF HEROIC BOOKS

Few things make me happier than meeting someone who has read my books or listened to my audiotapes and hearing something like, 'I was so moved and inspired after going through your material that I went out and bought ten more life improvement books and read them all. And you know what, they have completely transformed me.'

I not only write books on life leadership, I am a dedicated student of them. As I mentioned in an earlier lesson, I spend countless hours in large bookstores combing the shelves for the latest treasure that will enlighten and educate me. I also frequent used-book shops where I have picked up some of my most valuable books for only a few dollars (as I write this paragraph, I have a 'pre-owned' copy of Maxwell Maltz's classic *Psycho-Cybernetics* on my desk, which stills bears the sticker price of $2.95. Also on my desk is a copy of Seneca's *Letters from a Stoic*, a truly priceless work, which was purchased by my dad for $1.95).

While almost any reading will improve your mind, in a world where there is too much to do, you must be selective in the books you read. And so, I suggest you spend much of your time reading what Thoreau called 'The Heroic Books' – those books that contain 'the noblest recorded thoughts of man'. Let your mind drink deeply from the works of the great philosophers, such as Epictetus and Confucius. Study the poems of the wisest poets, such as Alfred Lord Tennyson, Emily Dickinson and John Keats, and the novels of Leo Tolstoy, Hermann Hesse and the Brontës. Read the writings of Mahatma Gandhi, Albert Einstein and Mother Teresa. Connecting with such works for even a few minutes a day will keep you centered on what life is really about and will ultimately profoundly affect your character. Asked in an interview what his biggest regret in life was, talk show superstar Larry King replied, 'I should have been better rooted in the great books.'

Here are some of the 'heroic' books that helped me change my own life and gave me the wisdom and inspiration to live more deliberately and completely. If you read all of them, and act on the lessons contained within their pages, you cannot help but improve your circumstances profoundly.

- *Letters from a Stoic*, Seneca
- *The Message of a Master*, John McDonald
- *Meditations*, Marcus Aurelius
- *The Autobiography of Benjamin Franklin*
- *University of Success*, Og Mandino
- *The Magic of Believing*, Claude Bristol

- *Siddhartha*, Hermann Hesse
- *Psycho-Cybernetics*, Maxwell Maltz
- *The Power of Your Subconscious Mind*, Joseph Murphy
- *As a Man Thinketh*, James Allen
- *Flow*, Mihaly Csikszentmihalyi
- *Think and Grow Rich*, Napoleon Hill
- *Life Is Tremendous*, Charlie Tremendous Jones

Through the wonders of technology, you can view a fuller listing of my favorite books at our website located at www. robinsharma.com.

44.

DEVELOP YOUR TALENTS

Norman Cousins once noted that 'The Tragedy of life is not death, but what we let die inside of us while we live.' In a similar vein, Ashley Montagu wrote that 'The deepest personal defeat suffered by human beings is constituted by the difference between what one was capable of becoming and what one has in fact become.' There is a difference between simply existing and truly living. There is a distinction between simply surviving and really thriving. The sad thing is that most people have lost sight of the human gifts that lie within them and have resigned themselves to spending the best years of their lives watching television in a subdivision.

In my speeches, I often use the following story drawn from ancient Indian mythology to remind the audience that there is an abundance of potential and ability just waiting to be awakened within us if we will only allow it to see the light of day. Thousands of years ago, it was believed that everyone who walked the earth was a god. But human-kind abused its limitless powers so the supreme god decided to hide the godhead, the source of all of this potential, so that no one could find it. The question then became, where could such a thing be hidden? The first adviser suggested it could be placed deep in the ground to which the supreme god replied, 'No, eventually someone will dig deep enough and find it.' The second adviser then offered, 'What if we place the godhead at the bottom of the deepest ocean' to which the supreme god responded, 'No, eventually some-one will dive deep enough and find it.' The third adviser then chimed in, 'Well, why don't we put it on the top of the highest mountain?' which prompted the supreme god to reply, 'No, I'm certain that eventually someone will scale that highest of peaks and find it.' After reflecting for some time, the supreme god found the solution: 'I will put this source of all human power, potential and purpose inside the hearts of every man, woman and child on the planet, for they will never think to look there.'

In all my work with employees of organizations across North America, I see the same thing: *too many people spend more time focusing on their weaknesses rather than develop-ing their strengths.* By concentrating on what they don't have, they neglect the talents they do have. The greatest people who have gone before us all had a simple strategy that ensured their success: they knew themselves. They made the time to reflect on their core abilities – those special qualities that made them unique – and spent the rest of their lives refining and expanding them. You see, we are all endowed with the capacity for genius. Perhaps you have just not taken the time to discover what your personal gifts are and then honed them to the level where you are considered brilliant.

Are you using the best within you to its fullest capacity? If not, you are not only doing yourself a disservice, you are doing the world, and all those within it who could benefit from your unique talents, a disservice. Ruskin put it this way, 'The weakest among us has a gift, however seemingly trivial, which is peculiar to him and which worthily used will be a gift also to his race.'

45.

CONNECT WITH NATURE

<< >>>

We live in an age of seemingly limitless information. The weekday edition of the *New York Times* contains more information than the average person was exposed to during an entire lifetime in seventeenth-century England. Over the years, I have found that spending time alone in natural surroundings connects me to the larger universe around me and restores my spirit in this hurried age.

After a busy week of speaking engagements, book signings and media appearances, the simple act of sitting in a wooded park and listening to the wind move through the leaves fills me with a sense of quiet and peace. My priorities become clearer, my obligations seem less pressing and my mind grows still. Communing with nature is also an excellent way to unlock your creativity and generate new ideas. Newton formulated the laws of gravity while relaxing under an apple tree. Likewise Swiss designer George de Mestral developed Velcro after examining the burdock burrs that clung to his dog while he hiked in the mountains. Natural surroundings serve to stifle the endless chatter that fills our minds so that our true brilliance can be liberated.

And while you spend time enjoying nature, observe your surroundings with deep concentration. Study the complexity of a flower or the way the current moves in a sparkling stream. Take your shoes off and feel the grass under your feet. Give silent thanks that you have the privilege of enjoying these special gifts of nature. Many people do not. As Mahatma Gandhi observed, 'When I admire the wonder of a sunset or the beauty of the moon, my soul expands in worship of the Creator.'

46.

USE YOUR
COMMUTE TIME

If you commute to the office for thirty minutes each way
every day, after one year you will have spent the equivalent
of six weeks of eight-hour days in your car. Given this, can
you really afford to spend all your time staring out the
window and daydreaming while the negative news blares
from the car radio?

So many of the highly successful and enlightened
people I know share a common habit: they listen to audiocassettes in their cars. In doing so, they transform their
driving time into learning time and make their automo-
biles moving universities. Turning your car into a 'college
on wheels' will be one of the best investments you will
ever make. Rather than arriving at work tired, frustrated
and dispirited, listening to educational audiocassettes
will make your commute fun and keep you inspired,
focused and alert to the endless opportunities around
you.

The best way to spot someone truly committed to life improvement is to ask him whether his car radio is working. The real students of effective living will have no clue because they spend every minute of their driving time listening to audio tapes. I cannot tell you how many times I have gone to get into the passenger seat of the car of a successful and fulfilled person and found a small mountain of tapes occupying the place where I was to sit. Most of the latest books can now be found on audiocassette along with many of the best motivational programs and life leadership systems. Personally, I try to listen to at least five new tapes a month ranging from the latest business bestsellers to programs on time management, creativity, positive thinking, physical well-being and spiritual satisfaction.

47.

GO ON A NEWS FAST

⟨⟨ ⟩⟩

Negative news sells. In our society, more people will choose to watch the criminal trial of a celebrity rather than the biography of a truly great human being. A newspaper with a headline revealing the latest tragedy will sell more copies than one announcing the latest scientific breakthrough. The real problem is that it is easy to get addicted to reading and watching negative news. I know so many people who begin their days by reading less than uplifting newspaper stories and who end them by catching up on the latest crimes, accidents and scandals on the late-night news.

I am not against newspapers or television by any stretch of the imagination. As a matter of fact, I find excellent information in many newspapers and have learned much from the intelligent TV programs I have watched over the years. My point is simply this: become more selective in the news you expose your mind to. Be more deliberate in the way you read your newspaper and in the way you watch your television. Before you start reading the morning paper, have a purpose in mind. Use it as an information tool to serve you and to make you wiser rather than as an excuse to help you pass time.

One of the best ways to wean yourself from the 'news addiction' that so many of us suffer from is to go on a seven-day news fast. Vow not to read even one negative story in the newspaper or watch even one negative news report on television for the next week. You will notice two things. First, you will not really miss out on much information. You will still hear about the most important stories of the day from the conversations that circulate around your office and through your encounters at home. Second, you will feel much more peaceful and serene. As well, you will find that the seven-day news fast offers yet another benefit: more time to do the things that will truly improve the quality of your life.

48.

GET SERIOUS ABOUT
SETTING GOALS

〈〈 〉〉

Many speakers and authors encourage you to set goals but most have never explained why this is such a powerful discipline beyond saying something like 'something magical happens when you write down your goals on paper.' In my opinion, setting clearly defined goals for all the areas of your life works for three reasons. First, it restores a sense of focus in your world, a world that has become complicated by too many options. In this age we live in, there are simply far too many things to do at any given time. There are too many distractions that compete for our attention. Goals clarify our desires and, in doing so, help us to focus on only those activities that will lead us to what we want.

Setting clearly defined goals provides you with a framework for smarter choices. If you know precisely where you are going, it becomes far easier to select those activities that will get you there. Writing down your goals clarifies your intentions (and the first step to realizing your vision is defining it). As novelist Saul Bellow once observed, 'A clear plan relieves you of the torment of choice.' Or as author Glenn Bland wrote, 'Goals and plans take the worry out of living.' If you set goals, the actions you take will be based on your life's mission rather than on your day-to-day moods.

The second reason that goal-setting works is that it keeps you alert to opportunities. The discipline almost magnetizes your mind to seek out new opportunities, opportunities that you need to seize in order to create the personal, professional and spiritual life you desire. And the third reason goal-setting works is that clearly defined goals commit you to a course of action. They give you the inspiration to act on your priorities and make things happen in your life rather than waiting for opportunities to land in your lap (which rarely happens). Selecting goals that engage and motivate you is one of the best ways to boost the level of your personal commitment to life and increase the energy you bring to your days. So set big goals. You are only as rich, whether materially or spiritually, as your dreams. Or as advertising genius David Ogilvy put it, 'Don't bunt. Aim out of the ballpark. Aim for the company of immortals.'

49.

REMEMBER THE
RULE OF 21

As I wrote in *The Monk Who Sold His Ferrari*, it takes about 21 days to develop a new habit. Yet most people give up on creating a positive life change after only the first few days when they experience the stress and pain that is always associated with replacing old behaviors with new ones. New habits are much like a new pair of shoes: for the first few days, they will feel uncomfortable. But if you break them in for about three weeks, they will fit like a second skin.

As human beings, we are genetically programmed to resist change and maintain a state of equilibrium. The condition, known as *homeostasis*, evolved naturally over time as a means by which our ancestors could survive constantly changing conditions. The problem is that the mechanism works to keep things as they are even when more favorable possibilities exist. And that is why we have such difficulty adopting new habits and overcoming the gravitational forces that prevent us from moving to higher levels of living.

But just as a rocket uses more fuel during the first few minutes after lift-off than it does over the days that follow when it will cover more than half a million miles, once you get past those first 21 days you will find that staying on course with a new habit will be far easier than you imagined. Take the time to study your personal habits and promise to make the necessary changes. The quality of your life will be determined in large measure by the nature of your habits. John Dryden observed, 'We first make our habits and then our habits make us,' while Virginia Woolf wrote, 'the skeleton of habit alone upholds the human frame.' So ensure that your habits move you forward rather than hold you back. In the timeless words of Publilius Syrus, 'Powerful indeed is the empire of habit.'

50.

PRACTICE FORGIVENESS

Forgiving someone who has wronged you is actually a self-ish act rather than a selfless one. Letting go of the hostility and hatred that you may have allowed to bottle up inside you is actually something you do for yourself rather than for the benefit of the other person. As I teach in my life-coaching programs, when you bear a grudge against some-one, it is almost as if you carry that person around on your back with you. He drains you of your energy, enthusiasm and peace of mind. But the moment you forgive him, you get him off your back and you can move on with the rest of your life.

Mark Twain wrote that, 'Forgiveness is the fragrance that the violet sheds on the heel that crushed it.' Forgiveness is a great act of spirit and personal courage. It is also one of the best ways to elevate the quality of your life. I have discovered that every minute you devote to thinking about someone who has wronged you is a minute you have stolen from a much worthier pursuit: attracting those people who will help you.

51.

DRINK FRESH
FRUIT JUICE

The foods you consume affect your moods as well as the clarity of your thinking. This is why the ancient sages ate only light foods. They knew that anything more would disturb the perfectly peaceful minds they had worked so hard to cultivate and disrupt their meditations on the true meaning of life.

If you owned an expensive Formula One race car, you wouldn't think of fuelling it with anything less than premium-grade gas. Anything else would reduce its performance. So why would you put anything less than the best foods into your body, which is an even more valuable performance vehicle? Eating the wrong foods, in large quantities, will reduce your energy level, affect your health and prevent your mind from serving you to its fullest capacity. Realizing that for every greasy lunch you have, you will suffer a corresponding reduction in your level of motivation and effectiveness is the first step to developing more disciplined eating habits.

One of the best strategies I can share with you to boost both your energy level and your mood is to get into the daily habit of drinking fresh fruit juice. On the counter of our kitchen at home sits one of my prized possessions, one that has added years to my life and life to my years: my juice machine. Investing in a juicer and discovering the life-giving value of fresh juice is a smart move. The juices you can make taste great and I cannot begin to describe how wonderful you will feel once you start drinking a glass of strawberry-apple or orange-grape juice every morning before you leave for work. The best book I have found on the subject of juicing is *The Juiceman's Power of Juicing* by Jay Kordich. The recipes Kordich shares in this book are worth the price alone.

52.

CREATE A PURE
ENVIRONMENT

One of the timeless truths of successful living can be stated simply: your thoughts form your world. What you focus on in your life grows, what you think about expands and what you dwell on determines your destiny. Life is a self-fulfilling prophecy – it gives you just about what you expect from it. As Helen Keller said, 'No pessimist ever discovered the secrets of the stars, or sailed to an uncharted land, or opened a new heaven to the human spirit.' Given this principle, the first step to becoming a happier, more serene person is to manage your thoughts and purify your thinking. One of the best ways to begin this inner work is to improve the quality of your personal environment.

After a speech I gave to a large gathering in San Francisco, an elderly woman slowly walked up to me and held my hand, as people in their golden years often do. Looking straight into my eyes she said, 'Mr. Sharma, I've listened to your insights for living a better life for the past hour and I agree with everything you've said. For many years I have understood that our surroundings shape our moods, our thoughts and our dreams. And so, in every room of my little house, I have a bouquet of freshly cut flowers. I am not a wealthy woman. But this is one luxury I would never do without.' This woman knew that a first-class environment is an investment, not an expense.

Take a good, hard look at your environment. Your thoughts are shaped by the people you associate with, by the books you read, by the words you speak and by your daily physical surroundings. Are you spending your time at work with negative people? If so, they will eventually make you negative and cynical. Are you watching violent TV shows and mindless videos at home? If so, your mind will grow restless and noisy. Is the space you work in bright, colorful and inspiring? Over the coming weeks, take steps to make the environment you work and live in a better one. You will quickly detect improvements in the way you think, feel and act.

53.

WALK IN THE WOODS

You will never go wrong by spending time enjoying nature. There is something particularly special about walking in the woods. Your steps will feel lighter, a deep sense of inner quiet will flood your entire body and your creativity will flourish. As the famed Italian architect and painter Leonardo da Vinci said, 'Through the window of the eye, the soul regards the world's beauty ... Who would believe that a small scene of nature could contain the images of the universe?'

My favorite time of year is autumn. The leaves on the trees reflect the brilliant colors of the season and it's the perfect time for long walks in the woods. Away from the noise of the city, the values I hold dearest grow clearer and I can contemplate some of life's larger questions, questions that never seem to get answered in the normal crush of the daily routine. I can stop by a small stream and relax on a moss-covered rock or inhale the fragrances that only those who walk in the woods truly experience.

When I leave this oasis of nature, I am a new man. I'm more alert, more energized and more alive. Many of the great wisdom traditions have emphasized the restorative power of regular walks in the woods. This life-giving discipline never fails to yield a bounty of welcome results.

54.

GET A COACH

One of the most effective ways to improve your personal and professional effectiveness and to rise to a new level of excellence is to find a mentor to coach you. Success in business and in life is a 'connect the dots' process. All you need to do is find out the habits, disciplines and strategies that others have used to obtain their results and connect the dots by duplicating their actions. Once you follow the steps they have taken, in the order they have taken them in, you are bound to get the same results. A personal coach can illuminate your path, encourage you when times get tough and shave years off your learning curve.

In my own life, I have been blessed with many mentors, people who have shown me the fundamentals of effective living and guided me in the right direction when I reached a crossroad. I found most of these special advisers by asking people whom I admired one of the most powerful questions in all of the English language, 'Would you please help me?' Not one of the people I approached refused to offer me the gift of their knowledge and the benefit of their experience. Many of my mentors have since become valued friends and my life would not be what it now is without them.

Coaching has become one of the most important elements to a complete program of personal and professional excellence. People from all walks of life have recognized this as one of the best ways to create positive changes and lasting results in their lives. As an executive in one of the monthly life-coaching programs I offer in cities across the country recently said, 'Inspirational books helped me to define my dreams. Being in your personal coaching program showed me precisely how to achieve them, while bringing back the balance in my life.'

55.

TAKE A MINI-VACATION

$$\ll \gg$$

While you cannot go on a major vacation every week, you certainly can go on a minor one. A mini-vacation begins with closing the door of your office, holding all calls and relaxing in your chair. Then close your eyes and begin taking deep breaths. Once you feel deeply at peace, begin to imagine you are at your favorite vacation spot. Vividly see the colors, hear the sounds and feel the emotions that this special place evokes. After only a few minutes of this mental escape, you will be rejuvenated, ready for the rest of the day ahead.

When I take my mini-vacations, I picture myself walking through a mountain meadow. I visualize my feet on the dewy grass and savor the splendor of the snow-capped mountains that frame this ideal scene. In the background, I hear the sound of water from a waterfall and imagine what the flowers that fill this field smell like.

Our minds are extremely potent devices. The subconscious mind cannot tell the difference between an image that we envision and one that is real. So this little technique actually fools it into thinking we are taking this quick break from our daily routines and invokes many of the wonderful physical benefits of a real vacation.

56.

BECOME A VOLUNTEER

I find a great deal of wisdom in the ancient Persian proverb 'I wept because I had no shoes until I saw a man who had no feet.' It is so easy to magnify our problems and lose sight of the many blessings we all have to be so very grateful for. Giving the gift of your time by volunteering to serve those who have less than you is an excellent way to remind yourself on a regular basis of the abundance that exists in your life.

After a keynote speech on leadership I delivered to the sales team of a large insurance company, a man came up to me and told me he was one of the firm's top producers. One of the reasons for his success, he said, was his habit of spending a few hours a week helping those less fortunate than he was. 'Seeing what others don't have keeps me awake to all the good things I do have. It prevents me from taking things for granted and, even more importantly, helps me make a difference in the lives of people who really need me.'

French physician Albert Schweitzer observed, 'I don't know what your destiny will be but one thing I do know: The only ones among you who will be happy are those who have sought and found how to serve.' And Anne Morrow Lindberg wrote, 'One can never pay in gratitude; one can only pay 'in kind' somewhere else in life.' Volunteering affords you the chance to help others and pay back the debt owed to those who have helped you.

57.

FIND YOUR SIX
DEGREES OF SEPARATION

In John Guare's play *Six Degrees of Separation*, the character Ouisa has a conversation with her daughter Tess in which she offers the following insight:

> I read somewhere that everybody on this planet is separated by only six people. Six degrees of separation. Between us and everybody else on this planet. The president of the United States. A gondolier in Venice. Fill in the names. I find that a) tremendously comforting that we're so close and b) like Chinese water torture that we're so close. Because you have to find the right six people to make the connection. It's a profound thought how every person is a new door, opening up into other worlds. Six degrees of separation between me and everyone else on this planet. But to find the right six people.

Ouisa was right. It is profound to think that you and I are separated from all the other people living on this planet by at most six people. She was also right in noting the real challenge: finding the right six people to connect you to the person you need to know.

One of the things I have done in my own life is to create what I call a Hero List, that is, a list of one hundred men and women I would most like to meet before I die. Since the law of attraction says that we attract into our life that which we focus on, this list is a tool I use to help me connect to the people I most admire. On more than one occasion, the Six Degrees of Separation principle has helped me find the right sequence of individuals who have led me to the person I've wanted to meet. And I am continually astounded by how many of the individuals on my list, which includes celebrities, business leaders, and other professional speakers, seem to cross my path in an airport or to be speaking at the same conference that I am or are having lunch at the same place that I am. The very act of listing my heroes seems to create a heightened sense of awareness that helps me spot them when they are close at hand.

58.

LISTEN TO MUSIC DAILY

In the most memorable scene of the wonderful movie *Jerry Maguire*, Tom Cruise's character, a hard-driving sports agent, has just signed up one of the hottest draft picks in football. As he drives away from the athlete's home in a state of utter joy, he impatiently searches from station to station on his car radio for the kind of song he can turn up loud and sing along to at the top of his lungs. Finally, to his great delight, he finds it – Tom Petty's hit 'Free Falling'. And he begins to sing his heart out.

Do you remember those times when you heard just the right song at just the right moment? Like Jerry Maguire, you started singing out loud and dancing with reckless abandon. In those moments, you felt fully alive, full of energy and truly happy. And all because you heard a few chords strung together in the right sequence. Music can do that to you. Music can lift your mood, put the smile back on your face and add immeasurably to your quality of life.

Get serious about listening to music that inspires you. Build a collection of your favorite pieces and play something that fills your heart with joy every single day of the week. For me, some moods call for a soothing piece of classical music or a soft jazz selection. When I'm writing a new book, for example, I will often listen to Johann Pachelbel's 'Canon in D' or jazz legend Chet Baker's "Round Midnight' compilation. If you have attended one of my seminars, you might have recognized the more upbeat music played before I step onto the stage. Even when I travel, I bring along my Walkman and listen to inspiring music such as the soundtracks to the movies *Braveheart* and *Everest* on the plane. Listening to even a few minutes of music every day is a simple yet exceptionally powerful way to manage your moods and remain at your best.

59.

WRITE A LEGACY
STATEMENT

Someone once said to me that the first fifty years of life are dedicated to building one's legitimacy while the last fifty are devoted to building one's legacy. How true. So many of us spend the first half of our lives striving for achievement and struggling to gain respect. Once we have this legitimacy, whether it comes in the form of prestige or material possessions, we soon realize that something is missing. We then spend the remaining years of our lives trying to do what we should have done from the beginning: create a legacy.

One day, my father posted a poem on the door of our fridge. It had been translated from Sanskrit and it read simply, 'Spring has past, summer has gone and winter is here. And the song that I meant to sing remains unsung. I have spent my days stringing and unstringing my instrument.' These words were written by a man whose heart was filled with regret over a life half lived. Rather than singing the great song he was destined to sing, he spent his days preparing and waiting until things were just right before he acted – 'stringing and unstringing his instrument', in his words. Sadly, that time never came.

The time to start building your legacy is today, not ten years from today when you 'have more time', because we both know that time will never arrive. Reflect on what it is you want to create in your life and, more importantly, what gift you wish to leave the world when you are no longer here. Greatness comes from beginning something that does not end with you. To help me see my own life's legacy more clearly, I have written a personal legacy statement. While many of the corporate executives I work with have personal mission statements, few have considered scripting individual legacy statements. While the former defines your vision of what you want to create while you live, the latter expresses what you aim to leave when you die. There is a distinction between the two. If you think about it, it will help you avoid feeling regret, sadness and disappointment about what could have been when you reach the end of your life.

60.

FIND THREE
GREAT FRIENDS

Cultivating great friendships is one of the surest ways to find more happiness and joy in your life. Recent studies show that those with a wide circle of friends and family live longer, laugh more and worry less. But friendships, like all other good things in life, take time, energy and commitment. Having said this, few things will offer greater rewards. As one philosopher wrote many centuries ago, 'There is nothing in the world more valuable than friendship. Those who banish it from their lives remove as it were the sun from the earth, because of all of nature's gifts, it is the most beautiful and the most pleasing.'

As I grew up, my father often said that the person with three great friends is a rich person indeed. I have never forgotten this advice and encourage you to take it to heart as well. To build deeper friendships, you must be willing to move out of your comfort zone, break the ice with people you might not know very well and show sincere warmth. If you plant the seeds of friendship, you are bound to receive a rich harvest of great friends. At a cocktail party, have the courage to walk over to someone you would like to get to know better and introduce yourself. Every human being has a deep need for affection and most people will be delighted you took the initiative. And if they do not respond to you, so what? Rather than viewing it as rejection, see it as their loss and politely move on to the next person who can benefit from all you have to offer.

A while ago, my mother's car had a flat tire while she was on her way to do an errand. She asked a stranger who was watering the lawn in front of her house whether she would mind if Mom left her car in their driveway while she walked to the gas station nearby to get help. The woman said she didn't mind and so my mother left. After returning and having the flat tire repaired, Mom went to the front door of the house and warmly thanked the owner for her kindness. The woman, in turn, invited my mother in for a cup of tea. Over the next hour, the two of them discovered they had grown up in the same town, gone to the same school and knew many of the same people. A great friendship developed simply because my mother took the initiative to make a new friend.

61.

READ *THE ARTIST'S WAY*

⟨⟨ ⟩⟩

We are all creative beings. When I first saw *The Artist's Way* on the shelf of my favorite bookstore years ago when I was still practicing law, I did not pick it up. At that time, I believed it was only for 'artists' and that I would, therefore, not benefit from it. Over time, however, I realized that every single one of us has an almost limitless wellspring of creativity deep within us. And we all need to use this creativity on a daily basis to get the most from life, whether we are lawyers, homemakers, teachers, business executives, poets or musicians. The realization that I, as a lawyer, was a creative being created a whole new awareness for me.

I started to attend seminars on creativity. I also read more books on the subject and searched for ways I could express this natural creativity to improve the way that I lived personally, professionally and spiritually. Eventually, my search led me to write my first book.

Read *The Artist's Way* and have the self-discipline to go through each of the thoughtful exercises the author, Julia Cameron, suggests you do. Unlocking your creative spirit will fuel your upward path of self-discovery and make every single one of your days far more fulfilling.

62.

LEARN TO MEDITATE

The French mathematician Blaise Pascal wrote, 'All man's miseries derive from not being able to sit quietly in a room alone.' We have become experts at filling our lives with noise and activities. We wake up to the sound of the radio blaring and dress while the television news is on. We drive to work listening to the latest traffic report and spend the next eight hours in a bustling office. When we come home, at the day's end, we delve into the evening's activities against the background sound of the television, ringing phones and humming computers. Pascal was right: most of our miseries do stem from the fact that we have lost sight of the importance of being silent, for even a short period, every day of our lives.

Without the ability to concentrate, a full and complete life is not possible. If you lack the mental focus to stay with one activity for any length of time, you will never be able to achieve your goals, build your dreams or enjoy life's process.

Without a disciplined mind, trivial thoughts and worries will nag at you and you will never have the capacity to immerse yourself in more meaningful pursuits. Without deep concentration, your mind will be your master rather than your servant.

My own life changed the day I learned to meditate. Meditation is not some New Age practice reserved for monks sitting atop mountains. On the contrary, meditation is an age-old technique that was developed by some of the world's wisest people to gain full control of the mind and, in doing so, to manifest its enormous potential for worthy pursuits. Meditation is a method to train your mind to function the way it was designed to function. And here's the key benefit: the peace and tranquility you will feel after twenty minutes of daily meditation will infuse every remaining minute of your day. You will be more patient in your relationships, more serene at the office and more happy when you are alone. Meditation will make you a far better parent, life partner, businessperson and friend. You cannot afford not to discover the power of this five-thousand-year-old mind training discipline.

63.

HAVE A LIVING
FUNERAL

<< >>

When I was doing research for *The Monk Who Sold His Ferrari*, I came across the story of an Indian maharaja who would engage in a bizarre morning ritual: every day, immediately after waking up, he would celebrate his own funeral, complete with music and flowers. All the while, he would chant, 'I have lived fully, I have lived fully, I have lived fully.'

When I first read this, I could not understand the purpose of this man's ritual. So I asked my father for some guidance. His reply was this: 'Son, what this maharaja is doing is connecting to his mortality every day of his life so he will live each day as if it were his last. His ritual is a very wise one and reminds him of the fact that time slips through our hands like grains of sand and the time to live life greatly is not tomorrow but today.' One's sense of mortality is a great source of wisdom.

While on his deathbed, Plato was asked by a friend to summarize his great life's work, *The Dialogues*. After much reflection, he replied in only two words: 'Practice dying.' The ancient thinkers had a saying that captured the point Plato made in other terms: 'Death ought to be right there before the eyes of those who are young just as much as before the eyes of those who are very old. Every day, therefore, should be regulated as if it were the one that brings up the rear, the one that rounds out and completes our lives.' Having a living funeral will reconnect you to the fact that time is a priceless commodity and the best time to live a richer, wiser and more fulfilling life is now.

64.

STOP COMPLAINING
AND START LIVING

Stop complaining about having no time for yourself and get up an hour earlier. You have the option, why not exercise it? Stop complaining about not being able to exercise given all that is on your plate these days. If you sleep seven hours a night and work eight hours every day, you still have more than sixty-three hours of free time every week to do all the things you want to do. This amounts to 252 hours every month and 3,024 hours every single year to spend on life's pursuits. There has never been a more exciting time to be alive in the history of the world and you have the choice to seize the boundless possibilities that every day presents.

If you are not as fulfilled or as happy or as prosperous or as peaceful as you know you could be, stop blaming your parents or the economy or your boss and take full responsibility for your circumstances. This will be the first step to a completely new way of looking at your life and the starting point of a better way to live. As George Bernard Shaw said, 'The people who get on in this world are the people who get up and look for the circumstances they want, and if they can't find them, make them.'

Make wiser choices about the thoughts you will allow to enter your mind, as well as the attitude you will bring to your days and the way you will spend the hours of your time. Stop complaining and start living. In the words of the poet Rudyard Kipling, 'If you can fill the unforgiving minute with sixty seconds' worth of distance run, yours is the earth and everything that's in it.'

65.

INCREASE YOUR VALUE

In the new economy you now find yourself in, you will be compensated not by how hard you work but by how much value you add to the world around you. Think about it. If you are currently being paid twenty dollars an hour, this money is being given to you not simply because you showed up at your desk for those sixty minutes but because you have added twenty dollars' worth of perceived value during those sixty minutes. So, the monetary reward you receive is determined not by how long you work but by how much value you add.

This is why a brain surgeon is paid so much more than a McDonald's employee. Is the brain surgeon a better person? Not necessarily. Is the brain surgeon a harder worker? Probably not. Is the brain surgeon smarter? Who knows? But one thing is certain: the brain surgeon has accumulated far more specialized knowledge and specific know-how than the McDonald's employee. There are far fewer people who can do what the brain surgeon does and, as a result, the brain surgeon is perceived as far more valuable to the marketplace. This is why the brain surgeon is paid over ten times more than the person who flips burgers. Money simply becomes a symbol for how much value each person has added to the world at large.

So to be paid more money in your work, you must add more value to the world. And the best way to begin adding value to the world is to start becoming a more valuable person. Acquire skills no one else has. Read books no one else is reading. Think thoughts no one else is thinking. Or, to put it another way, you cannot have all that you want if you remain the person you are. To get more from life, you need to be more in life.

66.

BE A BETTER PARENT

<< >>

The way you raise your children is the way you raise your future generations. Since few of us have had formal training in the fine art of parenting, most of us simply treat our children the way our parents treated us. We know of no other way to do it.

Although being a parent is a great joy, it is also a privilege that involves tremendous responsibility. While I would do anything for my two children, that willingness is not enough. We need to develop the skills of excellent parents. We cannot just hope that the way we are raising our kids is the right way and pray that we will be lucky enough that they become thoughtful, caring and wise adults. We must take the initiative to improve our parenting abilities by attending seminars, reading books and listening to audiocassettes by the leading thinkers in this field. Then we must have the courage to keep trying to refine the ideas we learn in the laboratory of our own lives in order to find the parenting strategies that best suit our families.

I know your life is busy and there is too much to do in too little time. But those miraculous years of your sons' and daughters' childhoods will never come again. And if you do not devote the time and effort to becoming the best parent you know you can be, one day you will deeply regret the lost opportunity. As one father who attended a seminar I gave in Toronto said, 'When my son was growing up, he constantly asked me to give him piggyback rides. Though I knew how much he loved them, I was always too busy to play with him. I had reports to read or meetings to attend or calls to make. Now that he has grown up and left our home, I have realized one thing: I would give anything in the world to give that little boy a piggyback ride.'

67.

BE UNORTHODOX

⟨⟨ ⟩⟩

Rousseau wrote, 'Take the course opposite to custom, you will almost always do well.' The brilliant ads for Apple computers inspire us to 'Think Different'. Or as I tell audiences at my leadership speeches, 'If you follow the crowd, the place you will most likely end up at is the exit.' To live a richer, more rewarding life, it is essential that you run your own race. Stop bending to the demands of social pressure at the expense of your uniqueness. When you study the lives of the world's most enlightened and effective people, you will see that they did not care about what other people thought of them. Rather than letting public opinion dictate their actions, they had the courage to let their hearts drive them. And in taking the road less traveled, they found success beyond their wildest dreams.

One of the best quotations about the importance of being unorthodox comes from Christopher Morley, who said, 'Read every day something no one else is reading.

Think every day something no one else is thinking. It is bad for the mind to be always part of unanimity.' And perhaps the very best one comes from Emerson: 'It is easy in the world to live after the world's opinion; it is easy in solitude to live after our own; but the great man is he who in the midst of the crowd keeps with perfect sweetness the independence of solitude.'

Over the next month, rethink the way you do things. Don't just do things because everyone else does them. Do the things that are right for you. Being different for all the right reasons is a wise way to live. Just ask Einstein, Picasso, Galileo or Beethoven.

68.

CARRY A GOAL CARD

<< >>

Time and time again, I have witnessed high-functioning, top-performing men and women carrying a little goal card in their wallets that they can review during the quieter moments of their day. The card simply lists their top life goals along with clear deadlines for achieving them. The discipline of reconnecting to your highest priorities, whether they are personal, professional or spiritual, is a smart one.

Montaigne said, 'The great and glorious masterpiece of men is to live to the point.' The wisdom of life so succinctly expressed. And yet most of us live our lives like one long air raid drill, filling our days with activities that seem important in the moment but that count for little in the overall scheme of our lives. As I wrote in *Leadership Wisdom from The Monk Who Sold His Ferrari*, the person who tries to do everything ultimately accomplishes nothing. Having a goal card and coming back to it three or four times a day will keep your mind centered on the things that truly count. It will foster the self-control you need to concentrate only on activities that advance your goals, give you the discipline to say no to all the rest and, in so doing, restore focus to your days. I promise you that if you spend your life focusing on only the worthiest pursuits, it is certain to end in complete joy.

69.

BE MORE THAN
YOUR MOODS

⟨⟨ᐧ ᐧ⟩⟩

For much of my life, I believed my thoughts were beyond my control. They just entered my mind automatically and did whatever they wished to do. Even worse, I believed that I was my thoughts. Thankfully, I discovered that nothing could be further from the truth. We are not our thoughts. Instead, we are the thinkers of our thoughts. We are the creators of the thoughts that flow through our minds and, given this fact, we can change our thoughts if we choose to do so.

This seemingly obvious insight was an epiphany for me. I soon became far more aware of the thoughts I allowed into my mind and the inner dialogue that takes place within every one of us every waking hour of every living day. I began to pay complete attention to the quality of my thoughts. This awareness was the first step to changing them. Over a matter of months, I trained my mind to focus only on positive, inspiring and enlightening thoughts. And in doing so, I saw the outer circumstances of my life change.

Just as you are not your thoughts, you are not your moods. You are the creator of the moods you experience, moods that you can change in a single instant. If you choose to do so, you can feel peace in a moment of stress, joy in a time of sadness and energy during a time of fatigue.

70.

SAVOR THE
SIMPLE STUFF

No one gets to take his possessions with him when he dies. I have yet to see a moving van following a hearse to a funeral. At the end of the day, the only thing we can take with us are our memories of all those great life experiences that add meaning to our lives. Given this, I would rather spend my days doing things that will leave me happy memories than collecting possessions.

I have discovered that my best memories come from life's simplest things. The day my daughter Bianca learned to walk, my son Colby's first Christmas concert (where he spent more time waving to his proud dad in the audience than singing the assigned song), the day our family played soccer in the rain and the evening we barbequed hot dogs under the full harvest moon.

Dale Carnegie wrote, 'One of the most tragic things I know about human nature is that all of us tend to put off living. We are all dreaming of some magical rose garden over the horizon instead of enjoying the roses that are blooming outside our windows today.' Have the wisdom to savor the simple things. The wonderful memories that they bring will add more value to your life than any of the material toys we spend so much life energy pursuing. As Emma Goldman noted, 'I'd rather have roses on my table than diamonds on my neck.'

71.

STOP CONDEMNING

Like the vice of complaining discussed earlier, it is easy to fall into the habit of condemning others, even those we love most. We criticize the way someone eats or the manner in which she speaks. We focus on the most minute details and find fault with the smallest of issues. But what we focus on grows. And if we keep focusing on a small weakness in someone, it will continue to grow in our minds until we perceive it to be a big problem in that person.

Would you really want to live in a world where everyone looked, acted and thought exactly as you do? It would be a pretty boring place. To live a happier, more peaceful life, begin to see that the richness of our society comes from its diversity. What makes relationships, communities and countries great are not the things that we have in common but the differences that make us unique. Rather than looking for things to criticize in those around you, why not begin to respect the differences?

Often, we perceive in others the weaknesses we most need to address within ourselves. Stop blaming and condemning. Accept complete responsibility for the way things are and resolve to work on changing yourself before seeking to change others. This is one of the truest measures of a person of strong character. As Erica Jong said, 'Take your life into your own hands and what happens? A terrible thing: no one to blame.'

72.

SEE YOUR DAY
AS YOUR LIFE

〈〈 ᐧᐧ 〉〉

'The days come and go like muffled and veiled figures sent from a distant, friendly party, but they say nothing, and if we do not use the gifts they bring, they carry them as silently away,' observed Emerson. As you live your days, so you will live your life. It is easy to get caught up in the trap of thinking that this day does not matter much given all the days that lie ahead of you. But a great life is nothing more than a series of great, well-lived days strung together like a beautiful necklace of pearls. Every day counts and contributes to the quality of the end result. The past is gone, the future is but a figment, so this day is really all you can own. Invest it wisely.

Your life is not a dress rehearsal. Lost opportunities rarely come again. Today, vow to increase your passion for living and multiply the commitment you will bring to each of the days that will follow this one. Many people think that it takes months and years to change your life. Respectfully,

I disagree. You change your life the second you make a decision from the depths of your heart to be a better, more dedicated human being. What takes the months and years are the efforts you must apply to maintain that decision. And the best life change decision you will ever make is the one to live every moment of your days to the fullest. As golf legend Ben Hogan said, 'As you walk down the fairway of life, you must smell the roses, for you only get to play one round.'

73.

CREATE A MASTER MIND ALLIANCE

In his brilliant book, *Think and Grow Rich*, self-help pioneer Napoleon Hill advises readers to form a 'mastermind' group if they aim to improve the quality of their lives and get what they want. He defines the mastermind alliance in these terms: 'Coordination of knowledge and effort, in a spirit of harmony, between two or more people, for the attainment of a definite purpose.' Hill adds, 'No two minds ever come together in a spirit of harmony without, thereby, creating a third, invisible, intangible force which may be likened to a third mind.'

Many of the successful people I personally coach or whom I have met at my seminars have told me that one of the single best things they did to help them create both the business and personal lives they wanted was to form their own mastermind alliance. In doing so, they not only developed a personal support network and some great friendships, they tapped into specialized knowledge and

ROBIN SHARMA

accumulated wisdom they ordinarily would never have had access to.

To form your own mastermind alliance, find three or four people you feel you could learn from and who would get along well with the others of the group. The alliance is all about mutual benefit so you must be able to give as much as you expect to receive. Approach your prospective members and arrange to start meeting once a week – early morning meetings are the best as they force each member to show his commitment to the group. With the advances in technology, you no longer have to meet in person although this will be important to do every so often. Telephone conference calls, electronic communication and even faxes will work. At the appointed time, discuss the challenges you are facing and ask for the group's input. Discuss the success principles and life lessons that have proved their effectiveness time and time again along with ways to live with greater balance, fulfillment and inner peace. A mastermind alliance will not only cut your learning curve in the game of life, it will help you have much more fun playing it.

74.

CREATE A DAILY
CODE OF CONDUCT

It is easy to live your life like a leaf in the fall wind, moving in whatever direction the wind blows that day. To create a great life, you must live more intentionally, deliberately and passionately so that you live on your own terms rather than on someone else's. The real challenge is that with so much to do, it is easy to allow life to act on you and watch the days quickly slip into weeks, then into months and finally into years. But I have a solution.

In my own life I have created what I call my Daily Code of Conduct. It is simply three paragraphs containing the values, virtues and vows I have determined through much reflection that I need to live by in order for my life to be a fulfilling one. For example, part of the first paragraph states, 'Over the next twenty-four hours I vow to appreciate this day, as it is all I really have, and to use every minute wisely and fully. So much can be done over the next twenty-four hours to advance my life's agenda and complete my legacy. I will, throughout this day, remember that this day could be my last and that no great person ever died with their music still within them.' My code then outlines my dearest values and vows as they relate to my family, my community and myself.

Reading my Daily Code of Conduct at the very beginning of the day, during the 'Base Camp' period I described in an earlier lesson, reminds me of the things that matter most in my life and reconnects me to my highest priorities, priorities that are so easily forgotten in the blur of daily events. After reading my code, I feel energized, committed and ready to go out into the world with a renewed sense of purpose and focus. Creating your own Daily Code of Conduct will do the same for you.

75.

IMAGINE A
RICHER REALITY

$\langle\langle \cdot \rangle\rangle$

Albert Camus once wrote, 'In the midst of winter, I found there was within me an invincible summer.' We really don't discover how powerful and resilient we are until we face some adversity that fills our minds with stress and our hearts with pain. Then we realize that we all have within us the courage and the capacity to handle even the greatest curves life may throw our way.

Many of the men and women who attend my leadership seminars come to me after the session and reveal the challenges they face in their lives. Some speak of difficulties they have motivating their employees in these uncertain times. Others speak of inner longings and the need to find a greater sense of meaning and fulfillment through their work. And still others ask me for advice on how to restore balance within their personal lives. My response always begins with the same lesson: to improve your life, you must first improve your thinking. Or as the old saying goes, 'We see the world, not as it is but as we are.'

Our greatest human endowment is the ability to reframe and reinterpret a difficult circumstance in a more enlightened and empowering way. Dogs cannot do this. Cats cannot do this. Monkeys cannot do this. This gift belongs only to us and is part of what makes us human. Blaming our circumstances for the way we feel is nothing more than excusing ourselves. In handling any problem, we must have the courage to assume a measure of responsibility for whatever situation we are in and then realize that we also have the capacity to use the setback to our advantage. Life's greatest setbacks always reveal life's biggest blessings.

76.

BECOME THE CEO
OF YOUR LIFE

〰️

'If it's going to be, it's up to me' is a wonderful mantra. I recently read in a newspaper that fully 10 percent of the population is betting they will win the lottery to finance their retirement. Too many people are leaving the quality of their futures to chance rather than to choice. It reminds me of the habit my brother had as a kid. When he saw that a glass was about to fall off a counter, rather than rushing to save it from falling, he would cover his ears with his hands so he could not hear it smash. (He has since grown up and become a Harvard-trained eye doctor, so his unique habit does not appear to have held him back all that much.)

This anecdote's point of wisdom is simply this: we need to keep our ears and eyes open to the realities of life. If we don't act on life and take action to make things happen, it will act on us and give us results we might not want. This is one of the natural laws that has governed humanity for thousands of years. To become more proactive during the weeks ahead, begin to see yourself as the chief executive officer of your destiny, the CEO of your life. All effective CEOs realize that 'if it's going to be, it's up to me' and act as the catalysts of their own dreams. Similarly, if you want something done, rather than waiting for luck to look your way, take steps to get it done. If there is someone you know could help you solve a problem or seize an opportunity, pick up the phone and call him or her. Remember, you can make excuses or you can make progress, but you cannot do both.

When I was practicing law, I would make a forty-five-minute journey on a commuter train to my office in a downtown tower. Every day, a man would sit in front of me who I came to see as a model of the Become the CEO of Your Life principle. Instead of sleeping or daydreaming like most of the other people on the train, this man decided to use his forty-five minutes to exercise. From the moment he sat down until the moment we arrived at the station, he would do arm stretches, neck rolls and a series of rigorous exercises to improve his health. Rather than joining the legion of people who complain they don't have enough time to work out, he took matters into his own hands and took charge of the opportunity. Sure he looked a little silly. But who cares what others think when you know that what you are doing is the right thing to do.

Seeing yourself as the CEO of your life can create a fundamental shift in the way you perceive your world. Instead of sailing through life as a passenger, you become the captain of the ship, leading things in the direction you choose to move in rather than reacting to the whim of the changing tides. And as you take greater control of your life, reflect on William James's inspiring words: 'Humankind's common instinct for reality has always held the world to be essentially a theater for heroism.'

77.

BE HUMBLE

One of the traits I respect most in people is humility. 'The tree that has the most fruit is the tree that bends to the ground,' my father taught me as I was growing up. And though there are some exceptions, I have found in my own experience that it is true – the people who know the most, who have achieved the most and who have lived the most are also the people closest to the ground. In a word, they are humble.

There is something special about being in the presence of a person who is humble. Practicing humility shows that you respect others and reminds us that there is so much for us yet to learn. It sends a signal to those around you that you are open to receiving the gift of their knowledge and listening to what they have to say.

I have had the privilege of meeting many famous people in my life. One of my biggest thrills was meeting the world champion boxer Muhammad Ali. Contrary to the cocky and loud image he cultivated in the media, in person he was a true gentleman and the very model of humility. When I had the good fortune to meet him in Los Angeles, he asked more questions about me than I asked about him. He spoke softly and radiated a warmth and decency that spoke volumes about the man he is. Muhammad Ali taught me that the more you are as a person, the less you need to prove yourself to others.

78

DON'T FINISH EVERY BOOK YOU START

〈〈 ‧ 〉〉

It is so easy to feel compelled to finish every book you start. A great sense of guilt fills our minds if we do not reach the end of that book we used our hard-earned dollars to buy. But not every book deserves to be read in its entirety. As Francis Bacon said, 'Some books are to be tasted, others to be swallowed, and some few to be chewed and digested: that is, some books are to be read only in parts, others to be read, but not curiously, and some few books to be read wholly, and with diligence and attention.'

I myself was guilty of feeling the need to read every book I picked up from beginning to end. I soon found that not only did my reading pile become unmanageable but I began to enjoy the pastime of reading less. Once I decided I would be more selective about which books I actually completed, I not only got through more of them, I found I learned more from each one.

If you find that after reading the first three chapters of a book, you have not gained any worthwhile information or that the book has failed to keep your attention, do yourself a favor: put the book away and make better use of your time (like reading the next book in your pile).

79.

DON'T BE SO
HARD ON YOURSELF

It is easy to spend much of your days beating up on yourself for past mistakes. We analyze that relationship that failed and relentlessly review all the things we did wrong. Or we look at that business decision that cost us so much and dwell on the things we could have done right. Once and for all stop being so hard on yourself. You are a human being and human beings have been designed to make mistakes. As long as you don't keep making the same errors and have the good judgement to let your past serve you, you will be on the right track. Accept them and move on. As Mark Twain wrote, 'we should be careful to get out of an experience only the wisdom that is in it – and stop there; lest we be like the cat that sits down on a hot stove lid. It will never sit down on a hot stove lid again – and that is well; but also it will never sit down on a cold one anymore.'

Coming to the realization that we all make mistakes and that they are essential to our growth and progress is liberating. We lose the need to be perfect and adopt a saner way of viewing our lives. We can begin to flow through life the way a mountain stream flows through a leafy forest, powerfully yet gracefully. We can finally be at peace with our true nature.

An excellent way to rise to a higher level of enlightenment and personal wisdom is to make a list of the ten biggest mistakes you have made in your life on the lefthand side of a page within your journal. Then, on the righthand side, write down the corresponding lessons you have learned from every mistake and the benefits that actually flowed into your life as a result of those so-called failures. You will soon see that your life would not be as rich and colorful without the mistakes of your past. So be gentler to yourself and see life for what it really is: a path of self-discovery, personal growth and lifelong learning.

80.

MAKE A VOW
OF SILENCE

〈〈 〉〉

The Buddhist monks have a favorite strategy to build will-power – one that has been used by many cultures over the years to create enormous amounts of inner strength and resolve. It is the vow of silence. Staying quiet for even short periods of time builds willpower and self-control because you exert force on your will by not giving in to the impulse to talk.

So many people talk far more than they have to. Rather than speaking precisely and communicating only what needs to be said, all too often we go on and on. This in itself reveals a lack of discipline. Discipline involves saying exactly what needs to be said and preserving your precious mental energy by not talking more than you have to. Measured, precise speech is also a sign of clear thought and of a serene mind.

A strategy that you can apply today to improve your personal discipline is to keep a vow of silence for one hour a day over the next seven. Don't speak at all during this silent time. Or if you must, speak only in direct response to a question and offer a clear, crisp answer rather than rattling on about everything from what was on TV last night to where you hope to vacation this summer. The vow of silence can be adopted politely and warmly. The idea is to make you stronger and to enhance your will, not to hinder your relationships. Within a matter of days, you will feel a sense of mastery and strength growing within you. Judge by the results: they will speak for themselves.

81.

DON'T PICK UP THE
PHONE EVERY TIME
IT RINGS

《 ﹥﹥

The telephone is there for your convenience, not for the convenience of your callers. Yet, as soon as we hear the phone ring, we act as if we are firefighters rushing to a five-alarm fire. We run to pick it up as if our lives depended on the call being answered at once. I have seen people interrupt quiet family dinners, dedicated reading times and meditation periods to answer those seemingly urgent phone calls, many of which turn out to be ones that could have been taken later.

Voice mail, though not perfect, is in many ways one of the great blessings of the modern age. It frees you up to do the things you want by allowing you to answer calls when it suits you. You no longer need be interrupted by the ringing phone and can spend your time on life's more important pursuits.

The habit of picking up the phone every time it rings is a hard one to break, as I know from personal experience. It is so easy to run to it, simply because we want to know who is calling us. Often, picking up the ringing phone is just another way to put off doing something you don't really want to do. But once you get good at letting it ring and staying focused on the activity at hand, whether it is reading a good book, having a heart-to-heart conversation with your life partner or frolicking with your kids, you will wonder what the hurry to pick up the phone was all about in the first place.

82.

REMEMBER THAT
RECREATION MUST
INVOLVE RE-CREATION

After a tiring day at work, it is so easy to curl up on the couch and spend the next three or four hours watching television. The irony is that, if you are like most people, you actually feel more fatigued after watching too much TV than you felt when you first sat down.

Recreation is tremendously important to a balanced life. But recreation must serve to re-create you. Recreation must restore you and bring you back to life. Real recreation will fill you with a renewed sense of optimism and energy. True recreation connects you to the highest and best within you while rekindling your inner fire. As Plato noted, 'My belief is not that the good body by any bodily excellence improves the soul, but, on the contrary, that the good soul, by her own excellence, improves the body as far as this may be possible.' Effective recreation then must involve some pursuit that soothes your soul.

83.

Choose Worthy
Opponents

〈〈 〉〉

I read recently that after Olympic athletes return home from the games, some of them suffer from what psychologists call POD (Post-Olympic Depression). After being in the world's spotlight and training for years to excel in competition, the athletes who suffer from this affliction fall into a state of depression once they get back to their daily lives. It seems that having achieved the pinnacle of success, there is no higher target for them to aim for and so life loses its meaning. A similar phenomenon was experienced by the *Apollo* astronauts who walked on the moon. After achieving this, they grew dejected at the realization that few things in life could match the excitement of traveling into space.

To maintain a healthy level of optimism and passion for life, you must keep on setting higher and higher goals. On attaining one goal, whether it is a career goal or a personal one, it is essential that you quickly set the next one. I call the process of setting progressively bigger, more engaging goals 'choosing worthy opponents'. When I was practicing law, I spent much of my time in courtrooms, representing the interests of my clients. Over the years that I argued these cases, I always found I performed best when I appeared against my toughest opponents. Those bright, highly prepared and exceptionally focused litigators forced me to get to the core issue before the judge and deliver my argument succinctly and effectively. The worthiest opponents compelled me to reach deep within myself and do even better than I had previously.

In the same way, selecting a steady stream of compelling goals will liberate the fullness of your talents. Remember, diamonds are created through steady pressure. So make certain your goals are worthy of you. Make sure they are the kind of challenges that will force you to reach into your heart and bring out the best within you, helping you grow in the process. In the personal coaching sessions I conduct around the country, many of the participants already have achieved what I would consider success in both their careers and lives. They are highly respected, influential and they enjoy what they do while leading balanced and fulfilling personal lives. Yet they join my programs because they know deep down that they can be more and that life holds greater rewards in store for them. They understand that in order to truly manifest their human potential and leave a legacy that lasts, they must keep raising the bar and holding themselves to a higher standard. And because of that attitude of constant improvement, life does send greater blessings their way.

84.

SLEEP LESS

〈〈 ˘ 〉〉

Thomas Edison's life story is one worth reading about. Part visionary, part gambler and part genius, he was a brilliant inventor who made the best use of his time on the planet. Though he had only six months of formal schooling, he had read such classics as *The Decline and Fall of the Roman Empire* by the time he was eight and invented the phonograph, which captured sound on records, by the time he was thirty. A master of positive thinking, when someone asked him why, during his last years when he was almost totally deaf, he did not invent a hearing aid, he replied, 'How much have you heard in the last twenty-four hours that you couldn't do without?' He then added with a smile, 'A man who has to shout can never tell a lie.' But what I remember the most about this special man was his rare ability to thrive on only four hours of sleep. 'Sleep is like a drug,' he explained. 'Take too much at a time and it makes you dopey. You lose time, vitality and opportunities.'

Most of us sleep far more than we need to. We say to ourselves that we must have at least eight good hours of time under the covers in order to function at our best. We cannot imagine getting by on less sleep and shudder at the very thought. Yet, as I wrote in an earlier lesson, it is not the quantity of sleep that is most important. What really counts is the *quality* and richness of your sleep.

Just remember those times when everything in your life was working. You were thriving at the office, fulfilled in your relationships and growing in your inner life. You were overflowing with energy and passionate about every minute of your days. If you are like most people, you will also recall that during these times you could get by on less sleep. As a matter of fact, there was so much to be excited about that you did not want to waste time by oversleeping. Now reflect on those times of your life when things were not going so well. Your job was exhausting, the people in your life were driving you crazy and you had no time for yourself. During these times, you probably slept longer than usual. Perhaps you slept until two o'clock in the afternoon on Saturday or Sunday (we often use sleep as an escape from reality during difficult times). But how did you feel when you finally woke up? Groggy, uninspired and tired.

So it is not the number of hours of sleep that is key but rather the amount of renewal your body receives. Strive for less time in bed but a richer, deeper sleep. Understand that fatigue is often a mental creation that stems from doing things you do not like to do. And remember Henry Wadsworth Longfellow's wise words:

The heights by great men reached and kept
Were not attained by sudden flight
But they, while their companions slept,
Were toiling upward in the night.

85.

HAVE A FAMILY MEALTIME

《 ‹ › ›

One of the many great family traditions my wonderful mother created for us when I was growing up was having a family meal every day. No matter what activities we had on the go, my father, my brother and I were duty-bound to come home for a dinner, where we could all reconnect and share our stories about the day that was drawing to a close.

My dad would often go around the dinner table and ask us to share one new thing we had learned. Or he would pull out a newspaper clipping he had tucked away in his shirt pocket and engage us in a lively discussion relating to the story. The special tradition of a daily family meal brought our family closer and gave me many happy memories. It is a tradition I have now brought into my own family life and one I hope my children will continue.

Your family meal does not have to be dinner. We live in busy times. We have endless personal commitments, our children have soccer practices, piano lessons and ballet classes, which might make it difficult to have a quiet meal in the early evening hours. Your family meal could take place over breakfast or lunch if your schedule allows for it. It might even be a quick snack of milk and cookies at the very end of the day. The important thing is that you find some time every day to 'break bread' with those you love most and consistently work at building a richer, more meaningful family life.

86.

BECOME AN IMPOSTER

<< >>

Research has shown that the way you act influences the thoughts you think. If you look to the ground, slouch over and generally model yourself physically after a depressed person, you will eventually start to feel depressed. If, on the other hand, you smile and laugh and stand upright with your head held high, you will soon find that you feel much better, even though you may not have been in a great mood to begin with.

Using this information, you can start to 'fake it till you make it'. In other words, you can pretend to be the kind of person you wish to be. By consistently acting as a highly enthusiastic person might or as a truly confident person would, you will eventually take on these personal attributes.

The power of the 'act like that which you most wish to become' technique was demonstrated by a study at Stanford University in which a team of psychologists took a group of emotionally secure college students and randomly separated them into two groups within a simulated prison setting. The first group was instructed to act like prison guards while the second group was told to take on the characteristics of inmates. The behavior of the group members was affected so dramatically by this experiment that the psychologists were forced to end it after only six days. The 'inmates' had become severely depressed, hysterical and suffered from crying bouts while the 'guards' behaved cruelly and uncaringly. As this study confirms, the 'acting as if' technique is a highly effective way to modify your behavior and transform yourself into the person you plan to be.

87.

TAKE A PUBLIC
SPEAKING COURSE

As a professional speaker who specializes in leadership, personal effectiveness and life improvement, I have the privilege of appearing on programs that feature some of the world's top experts like Brian Tracy, the renowned motivational speaker, Professor John Kotter, the respected business guru, celebrities like actor Christopher Reeve and musical superstars like Jewel. I give keynote addresses at about seventy-five major conferences a year and speak to large audiences across North America, in the Caribbean and in Asia. Yet very few people know that the greatest fear of my life was once public speaking.

While I was in school, I would avoid any opportunity to speak in front of people for fear of failure. If a teacher asked me to give an oral report to the class or speak on a certain subject, I would always find some excuse not to. My fear of public speaking affected my confidence and prevented me from doing many of the things I knew in my heart I could do. It was not until I took a public speaking course from the Dale Carnegie organization that I began to change. And once I did, a new world unfolded for me.

I have since discovered I was not alone in my fear. It has been reported that most people fear speaking in front of an audience even more than death itself. Talking to a large group of people draws us out of the circle of security that we tend to live in and forces us to confront an entirely foreign experience. But two things can dramatically reduce your fear of public speaking (as well as any other fear for that matter): preparation and practice. By taking a public speaking course that will prepare you for speaking before groups and offer you a regular forum to practice in front of a group, you will soon manage your fear and eventually master it.

88.

STOP THINKING
TINY THOUGHTS

The British statesman Benjamin Disraeli once said, 'Nurture your mind with great thoughts, for you will never go any higher than you think.' His words are profound. And his point of wisdom is clear: it is not what you are that is holding you back in life. It's what you think you're not. It is what is going on in your inner world that is preventing you from having all that you want. And the moment you fully understand this insight and set about ridding your mind of all its limiting thoughts, you will see almost immediate improvements in your personal circumstances.

In my motivational seminars, I tell my audiences, 'if you are not pursuing your dreams, you are fueling your limitations.' My brother, an internationally known eye surgeon, once told me about a medical condition called amblyopia, a condition that occurs when a patch is placed over a young child's healthy eye. When the patch is removed, the child has completely lost the sight of that once good eye. Covering the eye stunts its development and causes blindness. Many of us suffer from our own form of amblyopia. We go through life with blinders over our eyes, afraid to dream bigger dreams and do the things we fear. The result is always the same: like the child with amblyopia, we eventually lose our vision and spend the rest of our days within a very limited zone of movement.

Too many people lead small lives. Too many of us die at twenty and are buried at eighty. Remember, nothing can stop a person who refuses to be stopped. Most people don't really fail, they simply give up trying. And most of the limitations that hold you back from your dreams are self-imposed. So shed the shackles of 'tiny thinking', have the bravery to dream big for a change and accept that failure is not an option for you. As Seneca observed, 'It is not because things are difficult that we do not dare; it is because we do not dare that they are difficult.'

89.

DON'T WORRY ABOUT THINGS
YOU CAN'T CHANGE

Time and again, when I face a challenge in my own life, I return to *The Serenity Prayer* of Reinhold Niebuhr: 'God, give us the grace to accept with serenity the things that cannot be changed, courage to change the things which should be changed, and the wisdom to distinguish one from the other.'

One business executive who went through an exercise I use in my leadership coaching programs found that 54 percent of his worries related to things that would likely never happen; 26 percent were about past actions that could not be changed; 8 percent related to the opinions of people whose opinions really did not matter to him; 4 percent concerned personal health issues that he had since resolved; and only 6 percent concerned real issues worthy of his attention. By identifying and then letting go of the worries he could do nothing about or that were a complete waste of his energy, this man eliminated 94 percent of the problems that had plagued him.

90.

LEARN HOW TO WALK

Nearly ten years ago, I received a package in the mail from my father. In it was a worn-out old book that carried the following inscription on the inside front cover: 'Dear Robin, some time ago, I picked up this book from a store that sells secondhand books. Though the money paid for this book was nominal, its net worth is tremendous. I enjoyed reading it immensely and I hope you will too. Love, Dad.'

Published in 1946, the book is called *Getting the Most Out of Life* and is one of the treasures in my library of wisdom literature and self-help books. I have returned to the short essays it contains on a wide range of life improvement topics, bearing titles such as 'Wake Up and Live!' 'The Business of Living a Long Time' and 'How to Live on 24 Hours a Day', many times over the years and have grown much from the lessons offered. It is truly a priceless possession.

On a recent rainy day, I pulled out the book and flipped through the different chapters, stopping at the one entitled 'How to Take a Walk'. In it, author Alan Devoe shares his insights on how one can get the best out of walking. First, he advises, a walk should never have a specific purpose. Rather than having a destination, you should simply immerse yourself in the beauty of the walk itself. Second, you must never take your worries with you on the walk. Leave them at home, for if you don't, they will become even more deeply rooted in your mind by the end of the walk. And finally, be fully aware. Train yourself to pay complete attention to the sights, sounds and smells. Study the shape of the leaves on the trees. Observe the beauty of the clouds and the fragrance of the flowers. As he concludes: 'The world, after all, is not so unendurable, when a person gets a chance to look at it and smell it and feel its texture and be alone with it. This acquaintance with the world – this renewal of the magical happiness and wonderment which you felt when you were a child – such is the purpose of taking walks.'

91.

REWRITE YOUR
LIFE STORY

$\ll \cdot \gg$

One of the most wonderful things about time is the fact that you cannot waste it in advance. No matter how much time you have squandered in the past, the next hour that comes your way will be perfect, unspoiled and ready for you to make the very best of it. No matter what has happened to you in the past, your future is spotless. Realize that every dawn brings with it the corresponding opportunity to begin a completely new life. If you so choose, tomorrow can be the day that you start getting up earlier, reading more, exercising, eating well and worrying less. As author Ashleigh Brilliant has observed, 'At any moment I could start being more of the person I dream to be – but which moment should I choose?'

No one is stopping you from opening your journal and, on a blank page, rewriting the story of your life. This very minute, you can decide the way you would like it to unfold, change the central characters and create a new ending. The only question is will you choose to do so? Remember, it is never too late to become the person you have always wanted to be.

92.

PLANT A TREE

According to ancient Eastern thinking, to live a fulfilling life, you must do three things: have a son, write a book and plant a tree. By doing so, the thinking goes, you will have three legacies that will live on long after you die.

While there are clearly many more elements of a happy and complete life (I would add the joy of having a daughter to the list), the idea of planting a tree is an excellent one. Watching a tree grow from a sapling into a tall oak will keep you connected with the daily passage of time and the cycles of nature. Just as the tree grows and matures, so too will you be able to mark your personal passages and growth as a human being.

If you have children, you might also wish to plant a tree in honor of each of them. As they grow, you can carve notches on the trunk to mark their different ages. Each tree then becomes a living record of a different life stage. Planting a tree for each child in your family is a wonderful and creative act of love and one that your kids will remember for many years to come.

93.

FIND YOUR PLACE
OF PEACE

Everyone needs a sanctuary or a 'place of peace' where they
can go to be quiet and still. This special place will serve as
your oasis in a world of stress. It will be a spot where you
can take refuge from the crush of daily activities that
demand your time, energy and attention. Your sanctuary
does not need to be fancy. An unused bedroom or a corner
of an apartment with some freshly cut flowers on the table
will do nicely. Even a wooden bench in your favorite park
can serve as your place of peace.

When you feel you need some time alone, visit this sanctuary and do some of those 'inner development' activities
that are so easy to neglect during the course of a busy day.
Write in your journal or listen to a soothing piece of classical
music. Close your eyes and visualize your ideal day. Read
deeply from that book your mother always told you to read
or from a book of wisdom. Or simply do nothing for thirty
minutes and let the renewing power of solitude take hold.

Carving out a little time for yourself is not a selfish act. Replenishing your inner reserves allows you to give more, do more and be more for others. Making the time to care for your mind and spirit will keep you balanced, enthusiastic and youthful. And as L. F. Phelan once said, 'Youth is not a time of life; it is a state of mind. People grow old only by deserting their ideals and by outgrowing the consciousness of youth. Years wrinkle the skin, but to give up enthusiasm wrinkles the soul ... You are as old as your doubt, your fear, your despair. The way to keep young is to keep your faith young. Keep your self-confidence young. Keep your hope young.'

94.

TAKE MORE PICTURES

〈〈 ›〉

Every life is worth living. And given this, every life is worth recording. So often a friend will tell me about a breathtaking sight on a recent vacation or something hilarious his child did at the Christmas concert or about someone famous he has met. 'Did you get it on film?' I ask. 'I'd love to see the photo.' 'Next time,' comes the reply. 'I didn't have time to pick up a new roll. But let me try and describe what happened to you.'

A picture truly is worth a thousand words. Photographs capture and record life's greatest memories so that we can re-live them as the years go by. As I grew up, my father constantly took pictures of our family. Whether it was a family picnic, the first time I took his car out for a spin, or a simple gathering with friends, he was there taking pictures. Often, while he asked us to smile for the camera, I would grow impatient and gently ask him to take the photo quickly. 'You don't need to take so many photos, Dad,' I would say. 'What are we going to do with them all?'

Well now, as the years have quietly slipped by, I know what to do with all those photos. They have gone into albums that form part of the story of life's passage. They provide my own children with endless hours of amusement and offer our entire family a wonderful way to reflect on the simple things that have meant so much to us.

Take more pictures. Record the best times of your life. Collect photographs of the things that have made you smile or cry or appreciate the many blessings this world provides. Always carry a disposable camera in your car and two in your luggage when you travel. You might be surprised how good you will feel when you go through your albums years from now.

95.

BE AN ADVENTURER

⟨⟨ ⟩⟩

Teachers are climbing mountains. Entrepreneurs are flying hot-air balloons. Grandmothers are completing marathons and homemakers are taking up karate. The more routine our lives become, the greater our need to fill them with some real adventures. The more obligations that beg for our attention, the more important it becomes to shed those shackles of complacency and send our hearts soaring through some brave new pursuit.

'Man must not allow the clock and the calendar to blind him to the fact that each moment of his life is a miracle and a mystery,' wrote British novelist H. G. Wells. To connect more deeply to the miracles and the mysteries of your own life, vow to restore the spirit of adventure that you once knew as a child. Make a list of twelve pursuits you know would bring a greater sense of passion and energy to your normally mundane routine and tackle one of them every month for the next year. Doing so is a highly effective way to reinvent the way you live.

96.

DECOMPRESS BEFORE
YOU GO HOME

Ⓐ ⟨⟨ ⟩⟩

After a day of stress and pressure at the office, most of us arrive home cranky, tired and dispirited. We gave the best we had to our colleagues and customers and, sadly, we have nothing left for the people we love the most: our spouses, children and friends. Like gladiators who have just completed the battle of their lives, we wearily walk to our favorite easy chair and order family members to leave us alone until we regain our composure.

Taking ten minutes to decompress before you walk through the front door of your home will help you to avoid making this scenario a part of your daily routine. Rather than leaving work, driving home and rushing into your house, I recommend that you spend a few minutes sitting alone in your car while parked in the driveway. Use this time to relax and reflect on what you would like to accomplish during the next few hours with your family. Remind yourself how much your partner and children need you and how many fun things you can do if you simply put your mind to it. To further decompress, you could go for a quick walk around the block or listen to a favorite piece of classical music before you open the door and greet your family. Be creative about your personal decompression time and treat it as a chance to renew and recharge so you are the person your family wants you to be when you greet them.

97.

RESPECT YOUR INSTINCTS

$\langle\langle \rangle\rangle$

It is easy not to listen to what the Quakers call the 'still, small voice within', that inner guide that is your personal source of wisdom. It is often difficult to march to your own drum beat and listen to your instincts when the world around you pressures you to conform to its dictates. Yet, to find the fulfillment and abundance you seek, you must listen to those hunches and feelings that come to you when you most need them.

As I grow older, I give far greater respect to my instincts and to the natural reservoir of intuition that slumbers within each one of us. The impressions I receive when I first meet a new person or that inner sense of wisdom that softly nudges me in the right direction during a trying time have come to play a larger part in the way I work and live. It seems that with age comes the corresponding ability to trust your own instincts.

I have also found that my personal instincts grow stronger when I am living 'on purpose', that is to say, spending my days on activities that advance me along the path to my legacy. When you are doing the right things and living the way nature intended you to live, abilities you were not aware you had become engaged and you liberate the fullness of the person you really are. As the Indian philosopher Patanjali eloquently wrote:

When you are inspired by some great purpose, some extraordinary project, all of your thoughts break their bonds: Your mind transcends limitations, your consciousness expands in every direction, and you find yourself in a new, great and wonderful world. Dormant forces, faculties and talents become alive, and you discover yourself to be a greater person by far than you ever dreamed yourself to be.

98.

COLLECT QUOTES
THAT INSPIRE YOU

If you have read *The Monk Who Sold His Ferrari* or any of my other books, you know that I love using quotations from the world's great thinkers. I never knew why I loved these as much as I do until one of my mentors, after reading a manuscript I'd written, said, 'You love quotations for the same reason I do, Robin. A great quote contains a wealth of wisdom in a single line.'

So often in my readings, I come across just the right quote, which contains the ideal answer to a challenge I am facing. And my mentor was right. The value of a great quote does lie in the fact that it contains a world of wisdom, wisdom that may have taken the author many years to arrive at, in a line or two.

Over the next few weeks, start your own collection of quotations, words that you can keep referring to when you need some instant inspiration or advice about how to deal with those curves life sometimes sends our way. Another effective way that I use quotes is to paste them in places where I know I will see them throughout the day, such as on my bathroom mirror, on the refrigerator door, on the dashboard of my car and throughout my office. This simple discipline keeps me focused on what's essential during busy times, positive during trying times and centered on the principles of real success. On my personal computer, I have now collected hundreds of quotes from great leaders, thinkers, poets and philosophers on subjects such as how to deal with adversity, the meaning of life, the value of self-improvement, the importance of helping others, the power of our thoughts and the need for a strong character.

99.

LOVE YOUR WORK

〈〈 〉〉

One of the timeless secrets to a long, happy life is to love your work. The golden thread running through the lives of history's most satisfied people is that they all loved what they did for a living. When psychologist Vera John-Steiner interviewed one hundred creative people, she found they all had one thing in common: an intense passion for their work. Spending your days doing work that you find rewarding, intellectually challenging and fun will do more than all the spa vacations in the world to keep your spirits high and your heart engaged. Thomas Edison, a man who recorded 1,093 patents in his lifetime, ranging from the phonograph, the incandescent light bulb and the microphone to the movies, had this to say about his brilliant career at the end of his life, 'I never did a day's work in my life: it was all fun.'

When you love your job, you discover you will never have to work another day in your life. Your work will be play and the hours will slip away as quickly as they came. As novelist James Michener wrote:

> The master in the art of living makes little distinction between his work and his play, his labor and his leisure, his mind and his body, his information and his recreation, his life and his religion. He hardly knows which is which. He simply pursues his vision of excellence at whatever he does, leaving others to decide whether he is working or playing. To him, he is always doing both.

100.

SELFLESSLY SERVE

Albert Schweitzer said, 'There is no higher religion than human service. To work for the common good is the greatest creed.' And the ancient Chinese believed that 'a little fragrance always clings to the hand that gives you roses.' One of the greatest lessons for a highly fulfilling life is to rise from a life spent chasing success to one dedicated to finding significance. And the best way to create significance is to ask yourself one simple question, 'How may I serve?'

All great leaders, thinkers and humanitarians have abandoned selfish lives for selfless lives and, in doing so, found all the happiness, abundance and satisfaction they desired. They have all understood that all-important truth of humanity: you cannot pursue success; success ensues. It flows as the unintended but inevitable by-product of a life spent serving people and adding value to the world.

Mahatma Gandhi understood the service ethic better than most. In one memorable story from his life, he was traveling across India by train. As he left the car he had been riding in, one of his shoes fell to a place on the tracks well beyond his reach. Rather than worrying about getting it back, he did something that startled his traveling companions: he removed his other shoe and threw it to where the first one rested. When asked why he did this, Gandhi smiled and replied: 'Now the poor soul who finds the first one will have a pair that he can wear.'

101.

LIVE FULLY SO YOU
CAN DIE HAPPY

Most people don't discover what life is all about until just before they die. While we are young, we spend our days striving and keeping up with social expectations. We are so busy chasing life's big pleasures that we miss out on the little ones, like dancing barefoot in a park on a rainy day with our kids or planting a rose garden or watching the sun come up. We live in an age where we have conquered the highest of mountains but have yet to master our selves. We have taller buildings but shorter tempers, more possessions but less happiness, fuller minds but emptier lives.

Do not wait until you are on your deathbed to realize the meaning of life and the precious role you have to play within it. All too often, people attempt to live their lives backwards: they spend their days striving to get the things that will make them happy rather than having the wisdom to realize that happiness is not a place you reach but a state you create. Happiness and a life of deep fulfillment come when you commit yourself, from the very core of your soul, to spending your highest human talents on a purpose that makes a difference in others' lives. When all the clutter is stripped away from your life, its true meaning will become clear: to live for something more than yourself. Stated simply, the purpose of life is a life of purpose.

As this is the last of the life lessons it is my privilege to share with you in this book, I wish you a great life filled with wisdom, happiness and fulfillment. May your days be spent in work that is engaging, on pursuits that are inspiring and with people who are loving. I'd like to leave you with the following words of George Bernard Shaw, which capture the essence of this final lesson far better than I ever could:

This is the true joy in life, being used for a purpose recognized by yourself as a mighty one, being a true force of Nature instead of a feverish little clod of ailments and grievances complaining that the world will not devote itself to making you happy. I am of the opinion that my life belongs to the whole community, and, as long as I live, it is my privilege to do for it whatever I can.

I want to be thoroughly used up when I die. For the harder I work, the more I live. I rejoice in life for its own sake. Life is no brief candle to me. It's a sort of splendid torch which I've got to hold up for the moment and I want to make it burn as brightly as possible before handing it on to future generations.

ACKNOWLEDGMENTS

I express my deep appreciation to the entire team at HarperCollins. You folks have made publishing a wonderful experience for me. Special thanks to Claude Primeau for your wisdom, Iris Tupholme for your belief in this project, Judy Brunsek, Tom Best, Marie Campbell, David Millar, Lloyd Kelly, Doré Potter, Valerie Applebee, Neil Erickson and Nicole Langlois, my always insightful and highly competent editor. I also express sincere gratitude to all the sales reps who have supported my work from day one.

Thanks also go to Ed Carson, to my valued team at Sharma Leadership International for your energy, support and for managing my corporate seminar and media schedule while I was completing this book, to all the readers of my previous books who took the time to write to me and to my family for their abundance of love and kindness.

About Robin Sharma

Robin Sharma is one of the world's leading experts on leadership and personal success. His books, including *The Monk Who Sold His Ferrari* and *The Greatness Guide*, have topped bestseller lists across the globe and have been published in thirty-six countries – helping millions of people create extraordinary lives. His work has been embraced by celebrity CEOs, rock stars, top entrepreneurs and royalty. As well as being a much sought-after speaker, Robin is also a widely respected success coach for top businesspeople ready to be truly remarkable in all they do.

Robin is the CEO of Sharma Leadership International Inc., a premier training and coaching firm that helps people and organizations get to world class. Clients include Nike, BP, General Electric, NASA, FedEx, IBM and Microsoft.

robinsharma.com is one of the most popular resources on the Internet for leadership and success ideas, and offers

Robin's blog, robinsharmaTV, along with his acclaimed e-newsletter, The Robin Sharma Report.

To book Robin to speak at your next conference or to discover more of his ideas, visit robinsharma.com today.

Now read this extract from Robin Sharma's ground-breaking book

THE MONK WHO SOLD HIS FERRARI

1.

THE WAKE-UP CALL

He collapsed right in the middle of a packed courtroom. He was one of this country's most distinguished trial lawyers. He was also a man who was as well known for the three-thousand-dollar Italian suits that draped his well-fed frame as for his remarkable string of legal victories. I simply stood there, paralyzed by the shock of what I had just witnessed. The great Julian Mantle had been reduced to a victim and was now squirming on the ground like a helpless infant, shaking and shivering and sweating like a maniac.

Everything seemed to move in slow motion from that point on. 'My God, Julian's in trouble!' his paralegal screamed, emotionally offering us a blinding glimpse of the obvious. The judge looked panic-stricken and quickly muttered something into the private phone she had had installed in the event of an emergency. As for me, I could only stand there, dazed and confused. *Please don't die, you old fool. It's too early for you to check out. You don't deserve to die like this.*

The bailiff, who earlier had looked as if he had been embalmed in his standing position, leapt into action and started to perform CPR on the fallen legal hero. The paralegal was at his side, her long blonde curls dangling over Julian's ruby-red face, offering him soft words of comfort, words that he obviously could not hear.

I had known Julian for seventeen years. We had first met when I was a young law student hired by one of his partners as a summer research intern. Back then, he'd had it all. He was a brilliant, handsome and fearless trial attorney with dreams of greatness. Julian was the firm's young star, the rain-maker in waiting. I can still remember walking by his regal corner office while I was working late one night and stealing a glimpse of the framed quotation perched on his massive oak desk. It was by Winston Churchill and it spoke volumes about the man that Julian was:

> Sure I am that this day we are masters of our fate, that the task which has been set before us is not above our strength; that its pangs and toils are not beyond my endurance. As long as we have faith in our own cause and an unconquerable will to win, victory will not be denied us.

Julian also walked his talk. He was tough, hard-driving and willing to work eighteen-hour days for the success he believed was his destiny. I heard through the grapevine that his grandfather had been a prominent senator and his father a highly respected judge of the Federal Court. It was obvious that he came from money and that there were enormous expectations weighing on his Armaniclad shoulders. I'll admit one thing though: he ran his own race. He was determined to do things his own way – and he loved to put on a show.

Julian's outrageous courtroom theatrics regularly made the front pages of the newspapers. The rich and famous flocked to his side whenever they needed a superb legal tactician with an aggressive edge. His extracurricular activities were probably as well known. Latenight visits to the city's finest restaurants with sexy young fashion models, or reckless drinking escapades with the rowdy band of brokers he called his 'demolition team', became the stuff of legend at the firm.

I still can't figure out why he picked me to work with him on that sensational murder case he was to argue that first summer. Though I had graduated from Harvard Law School, his alma mater, I certainly wasn't the brightest intern at the firm, and my family pedigree reflected no blue blood. My father spent his whole life as a security guard with a local bank after a stint in the Marines. My mother grew up unceremoniously in the Bronx.

Yet he did pick me over all the others who had been quietly lobbying him for the privilege of being his legal gofer on what became known as 'the Mother of All Murder Trials': he said he liked my 'hunger'. We won, of course, and the business executive who had been charged with brutally killing his wife was now a free man – or as free as his cluttered conscience would let him be.

My own education that summer was a rich one. It was far more than a lesson on how to raise a reasonable doubt where none existed – any lawyer worth his salt could do that. This was a lesson in the psychology of winning and a rare opportunity to watch a master in action. I soaked it up like a sponge.

At Julian's invitation, I stayed on at the firm as an associate, and a lasting friendship quickly developed between us. I will admit that he wasn't the easiest lawyer to work with. Serving as his junior was often an exercise in frustration, leading to more than a few late-night shouting matches. It was truly his way or the highway. This man could never be wrong. However, beneath his crusty exterior was a person who clearly cared about people.

No matter how busy he was, he would always ask about Jenny, the woman I still call 'my bride' even though we were married before I went to law school. On finding out from another summer intern that I was in a financial squeeze, Julian arranged for me to receive a generous scholarship. Sure, he could play hardball with the best of them, and sure, he loved to have a wild time, but he never neglected his friends. The real problem was that Julian was obsessed with work.

For the first few years he justified his long hours by saying that he was 'doing it for the good of the firm', and that he planned to take a month off and go to the Caymans '*next* winter for sure'. As time passed, however, Julian's reputation for brilliance spread and his workload continued to increase. The cases just kept on getting bigger and better, and Julian, never one to back down from a good challenge, continued to push himself harder and harder. In his rare moments of quiet, he confided that he could no longer sleep for more than a couple of hours without waking up feeling guilty that he was not working on a file. It soon became clear to me that he was being consumed by the hunger for more: more prestige, more glory and more money.

As expected, Julian became enormously successful. He achieved everything most people could ever want: a stellar professional reputation with an income in seven figures, a spectacular mansion in a neighborhood favored by celebrities, a private jet, a summer home on a tropical island and his prized possession – a shiny red Ferrari parked in the center of his driveway.

Yet I knew that things were not as idyllic as they appeared on the surface. I observed the signs of impending doom not because I was so much more perceptive than the others at the firm, but simply because I spent the most time with the man. We were always together because we were always at work. Things never seemed to slow down. There was always another blockbuster case on the horizon that was bigger than the last. No amount of preparation was ever enough for Julian. What would happen if the judge brought up this question or that question, God forbid? What would happen if our research was less than perfect? What would happen if he was surprised in the middle of a packed courtroom, looking like a deer caught in the glare of an intruding pair of headlights? So we pushed ourselves to the limit and I got sucked into his little work-centered world as well. There we were, two slaves to the clock, toiling away on the sixty-fourth floor of some steel and glass monolith while most sane people were at home with their families, thinking we had the world by the tail, blinded by an illusory version of success.

The more time I spent with Julian, the more I could see that he was driving himself deeper into the ground. It was as if he had some kind of a death wish. Nothing ever satisfied him. Eventually, his marriage failed, he no longer spoke with his father, and though he had every material possession anyone could want, he still had not found whatever it was that he was looking for. It showed, emotionally, physically – and spiritually.

At fifty-three years of age, Julian looked as if he was in his late seventies. His face was a mass of wrinkles, a less than glorious tribute to his 'take-no-prisoners' approach to life in general and the tremendous stress of his out-ofbalance lifestyle in particular. The late-night dinners in expensive French restaurants, smoking thick Cuban cigars and drinking cognac after cognac, had left him embarrassingly overweight. He constantly complained that he was sick and tired of being sick and tired. He had lost his sense of humor and never seemed to laugh anymore. Julian's once enthusiastic nature had been replaced by a deathly somberness. Personally, I think that his life had lost all purpose.

Perhaps the saddest thing was that he had also lost his focus in the courtroom. Where he would once dazzle all those present with an eloquent and airtight closing argument, he now droned on for hours, rambling about obscure cases that had little or no bearing on the matter before the Court. Where once he would react gracefully to the objections of opposing counsel, he now displayed a biting sarcasm that severely tested the patience of judges who had earlier viewed him as a legal genius. Simply put, Julian's spark of life had begun to flicker.

It wasn't just the strain of his frenetic pace that was marking him for an early grave. I sensed it went far deeper. It seemed to be a spiritual thing. Almost every day he would tell me that he felt no passion for what he was doing and was enveloped by emptiness. Julian said that as a young lawyer he really loved the Law, even though he was initially pushed into it by the social agenda of his family. The Law's complexities and intellectual challenges had kept him spellbound and full of energy. Its power to effect social change had inspired and motivated him. Back then, he was more than just some rich kid from Connecticut. He really saw himself as a force for good, an instrument for social improvement who could use his obvious gifts to help others. That vision gave his life meaning. It gave him a purpose and it fuelled his hopes.

There was even more to Julian's undoing than a rusty connection to what he did for a living. He had suffered some great tragedy before I had joined the firm. Something truly unspeakable had happened to him, according to one of the senior partners, but I couldn't get anyone to open up about it. Even old man Harding, the notoriously loose-lipped managing partner who spent more time in the bar of the Ritz-Carlton than in his embarrassingly large office, said that he was sworn to secrecy. Whatever this deep, dark secret was, I had a suspicion that it, in some way, was contributing to Julian's downward spiral. Sure I was curious, but most of all, I wanted to help him. He was not only my mentor; he was my best friend.

And then it happened. This massive heart attack that brought the brilliant Julian Mantle back down to earth and reconnected him to his mortality. Right in the middle of courtroom number seven on a Monday morning, the same courtroom where we had won the Mother of All Murder Trials.

Also by
Robin Sharma

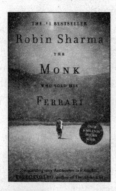

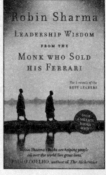

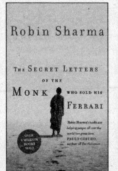

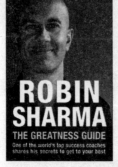

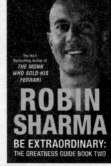